A BIRDWATCH
EASTEI

CW00349776

by
MALCOLM PALMER
with
LUIS FIDEL

ARLEQUIN PRESS

ISBN 1 900159 66 X

Published 2001

Arlequin Press, 26 Broomfield Road, Chelmsford, Essex CM1 1SW
Telephone: 01245 267771
www.arlequinpress.co.uk
© Malcolm Palmer/Arlequin Press

A catalogue record for this book is available.

Photographs by Luis Fidel and Sergio Arroyo.
Cover and vignettes by John Busby.

To Maria

Acknowledgements

Help in the production of this guide has come from many sources, and it is to be regretted that not everyone who has submitted observations and assistance of many kinds will be mentioned here, but special thanks are due to José Aragoneses, Brian Conduit, José Damian Navarro, Antonio Jacobo Ramós and John Robinson for their many observations. Our long-suffering 'better-halves', Juanita and Susi, must also be thanked for their forbearance, as well as Javier Falco for help with computing.

Essentially, in the case of any guide of this type, much literature has to be consulted, and the main publications from which information has been gleaned, are listed below:–

Handbook of the Birds of Europe ('BWP'), edited by Stanley Cramp – OUP

Atlas de las Aves de España (1975-1995), SEO – Lynx Edicions

Atlas de las Aves Nidificantes de la Comunidad Valenciana, Urios *et al* – Generalitat Valenciana.

Donde Ver Aves en España Peninsular, SEO – Lynx

Las Aves de los Humedales del Sur de Alicante, Ramos & Fidel – ECU

Estudio Ornitológico de 'El Hondo,' Navarro – CAM

Estudio ecológico de la laguna de La Mata, Calvo & Iborra – Instituto Gil-Albert

Áreas Importantes para las Aves en España, SEO

Fauna de Aragón: Las aves. – Aragües & Lucientes – Guara Editorial

On Observar Ocells a Catalunya, Del Hoyo & Sargatal – Lynx

Las Aves Marinas de España y Portugal, Patterson – Lynx

Anuarios Ornitológicos de la Comunidad Valenciana, Dies & Dies – Estació Ornitológico de la Albufera.

Anuaris d'Ornitologia de Catalunya, Grup Catalá d'Anellament – SEO *et al*

'Ardeola' & 'Garcilla' – Magazines published by the SEO, including annual rarities reports.

Information has also been drawn from magazines and reviews, such as 'El Bruel' – a bulletin produced by the 'Friends of Aiguamolls' and 'La Matruca' – published by the 'Friends of the

Alicante Wetlands.' Such organizations, many penniless and still embryonic, are worthy of your support.

A list of useful addresses and telephone numbers follows:-

Parque natural de El Hondo, Vereda de Sendres s/n, 03295 Elche, tel. 96-667-85-15

P. n. de las Salinas de Santa Pola, tel. 96-669-35-46

P. n. de la Mata/Torrevieja, casa Forestal de la Mata, 03188 La Mata, tel. 96-692-04-04

P. n. de la Font Roja, Ctra de la Font Roja s/n, 03800 Alcoy, tel. 96-533-76-20

P. n. del Peñon de Ifach, tel. 96-597-20-15

P. n. del Montgo, tel. 96-642-32-05

P. n. de la marjal de Pego, C/San Agusti, 6-2°, 03780 Pego, tel. 96-640-02-51

P. n. de l'Albufera, Raco de l'Olla, Ctra del Palmar, s/n, 46012, Valencia, tel. 96-162-73-45

P.n. de Cabanes-Torreblanca, C. Experimental d'Aqüicultura, Ribera de Cabanes, 12180 Cabanes, tel. 908-04-84-31

Reserva natural de les Illes Columbretes, Planetari de Castelló, Passeig Maritim, 1, 12100, Grau de Castelló, tel 96-428-29-68

Laguna de Gallocanta, Albergur Rural Ornitológico 'Allucant' San Vicent s/n, 50373 Gallocanta, Zaragoza, tel 97-680-31-37

P.n. de Aiguamolls, tel. 972-25-03-22

Delta de Llobregat, CISEN, tel. 93-478-39-88
P.n. de Montserrat, 93-835-02-51
Delta del Ebro, 977-48-96-79

For general information:–
SEO/Birdlife,
C/Melquiades Biencinto, 34,
28053 Madrid, tel 91-434-09-10.

Note: Many of the above telephones will have at their disposal someone with at least some knowledge of English, though you may have to ring back at a particular time.

CONTENTS

Introduction

I wrote my 'Birdwatching Guide to the Costa Blanca' some years ago, and it was, of course, immediately out-of-date. 'Of course' because all such volumes suffer from the constantly changing patterns of bird-distribution – and observer-distribution! Hopefully, authors also evolve, as they learn more of the area they study.

The scope of the earlier guide was strictly limited, covering only those sites within the boundaries of Alicante Province. As I travelled wider within this under-watched and infinitely varied country, I quickly became aware that more of the coastal region to the north, and its mountainous hinterland, needed introducing to the itinerant ornithologist.

It also soon became obvious that this was no undertaking for one person alone, and I enlisted the help of Luis Fidel Sarmiento. Luis is author of a work on the wetlands of the region, and, in his official capacity, is responsible for environmental protection in the south of Alicante. He is also able to read Catalán, a skill which has proved invaluable in translating much material emanating from those independent regions. So we have produced a colaborative work. The writing is all mine, so I plead guilty to all errors and ommissions you may come across, but much of the research has been carried out by Luis, without whose help this book could not have been written.

Probably unusually for a book of this type, the specific list represents an attempt to pull together all existing information on the birds of the region, so it is to be hoped that it can be regarded as a 'check-list' – although records, especially from inland areas, are patchy.

As ornithology develops as both a science and a pastime amongst the Spanish, so will the species-list grow, but I trust this book will at least provide an insight into the birdlife you are likely, as a visitor, to encounter, at any given season. There can be few areas of Europe with more diversity of habitat available for distance covered, and the sensitive species found here are many and exciting. Enjoy it!

Malcolm Palmer, Santa Pola, 2001.

Travel and Practical Information

Getting there

Because of the continuing popularity of package deal holidays, and the increasing number of Northern Europeans who own property in South-east Spain, there is a huge range of flights available to the airports serving the region covered, particularly Alicante, to where charter flights can often be obtained at bargain prices. Although frequently subject to irritating delays, these charters represent the cheapest and quickest means of getting to Mediterranean birds currently available. Scheduled flights are also an option, and both Iberia and Monarch have regular services to Alicante, from Heathrow and Luton respectively.

Reus also has a regular service of charters, whist Valencia has a scheduled service from Heathrow, as does Barcelona. Girona, particularly in summer, carries a good number of charters.

If you wish to come by road, prepare for a long drive. perhaps the best route is via Portsmouth-Caen, then down the west coast of France, across the Pyrenees, and down through Zaragoza. The long-distance ferries plying between Portsmouth and Bilbao, and Plymouth-Santander are another option, and there have been many reports of some good sea-birds seen on these crossings. They are, however, not for the weak of stomach, as Biscay can be a touch 'interesting!' The sheer fact of the matter is that, economically, the driving option is a non-starter, and is even less attractive if your holiday time is limited. You can hire a decent vehicle, with left-hand-drive, of course, at any of the airports, at quite reasonable rates, and the cost of the air-fare plus car-hire will probably be less than your costs in driving down. However, if you have lots of time, and wish to see some of the great birding areas of France, it's a different matter.

Driving on Spanish roads

To drive safely on Spanish roads, it is necessary, as in other parts of the world, to drive 'defensively' – that is, to assume that the other fellow is going to do something daft. People with M (for Madrid) plates have a deserved reputation for foolhardy driving, and patience, as elsewhere, is not a property of the young. A strange dichotomy in the Spanish character dictates that the same guy who cuts you up mercilessly on the open road, will wait patiently while you stop in front of him in a narrow street, to buy a lottery ticket, or disgorge Granny and the kids.

As to rules: Always wear your seat-belts, especially in the front, never cross a solid white line in the centre of the road, or turn left when there is no box from which to do so (except on very minor roads), never stop with your wheels on the carriageway, especially if there is a solid white line down the side, and always observe speed-limits. Failure to comply with any of the above can result in a hefty on-the-spot fine. If you don't have the money on you, the nice kind policeman will insist that you accompany him to the nearest cashpoint to obtain it. Further lack of compliance will see your car impounded until you are able to pay.

Parking in towns is OK anywhere where there is no prohibition, and this can take the form of a 'Vado permanente' – or entrance with a blue and red sign and a certificate number, issued by the Town Hall. Your car will be towed away for an infringement, and you will have to call at the Local Police Station to retrieve it. The local police wear blue uniforms and are usually not quite so strict as the Guardia Civil, who are responsible for all traffic outside towns, and who will happily breathalise you if they wish. Again the fines are heavy. All police are normally polite to foreigners – return this in kind, and you may get away with a small infraction!

Maps are available in many forms, the Michelin series being the best for motoring in general, with a series of road maps which cover Spain in seven sheets. More detailed maps may be obtained from good map shops, such as Stanford's, in Leicester Square, but, except in the tourist areas, these larger-scale works tend to be out of date military affairs.

Road atlases are available at all garages, as the petrol companies publish their own.

Petrol is, at the time of writing, considerably cheaper than it is in Britain, but diesel is the best buy – 20% cheaper than petrol. Be careful that you are aware that diesel may be known as such, or as 'gasoleo' – petrol is available in 'Super' or 'Sin plomo'- lead-free. Most garages are not self-service, but some newer ones are. Until a few years ago, petrol was a monopoly, but now you will see all the brands you encounter elsewhere.

Car Hire

The major international hire companies are well-represented at all the airports, but you will get a much better deal if you book a car in advance, either when you buy your flight, or through someone you know in Spain. The smaller companies will always be cheaper, and many of them have a wide range of vehicles. Try to resist the temptation to hire an open-top jeep, unless you enjoy being fried, and choked with dust. Insist on unlimited mileage, and remove any tell-tale stickers from the car, which merely announce that this vehicle is available to be broken into!

Package Holidays

It is likely that many birders will visit the region as part of a family holiday, with their spouses and/or offspring insisting on a fair amount of sightseeing/sunbathing. It is possible to see lots of birds in this way, with just a little planning – and patience!

Anyone interested in a birding package holiday would be well-advised to call Calandra Holidays, on 01223-872107 – they can also fix up for car-hire, and advise on a wide range of holiday options.

Security

NEVER leave anything on view in a car, especially a hire-car, or one with foreign plates. Theft from cars, as in most countries, is rife. Motorway service areas are particularly risky, and camper-vans are a favourite target (as well as being an utter pain on the roads!). A nasty type of crime which has been reported is for a car to flag you down, pointing out some imaginary fault in your car. You stop, and someone helps themselves from your vehicle whilst you are looking under the bonnet. Away from cars, take normal precautions with your belongings, and avoid carrying large amounts of cash. Muggings are rare, outside 'bad' areas of Barcelona, for instance, and pickpocketing is much more common, especially around street-markets. Hotels will look after your valuables, if requested.

Hazards

There are remarkably few natural hazards in this part of the world. Snakes are virtually all harmless. The rare Lataste's Viper is more commonly found further south and west, but is aggressive and quite venomous (though rarely fatal). The Montpellier Snake is venomous but back-fanged, and unable to bite you unless you put a finger in its mouth – don't! There are scorpions, which live under rocks, and can sting nastily, and tarantulas, which are largely nocturnal and shy of human beings. Bulls and, rarely, wild boar, are capable of putting you to flight, but none of the above is as pestilential as the mosquito. These abound, especially in spring, and in the evenings they can be a menace. They will bite through anything, and there are few preparations that give more than token protection, but they are nowhere near so much of a problem as they are in more northerly lattitudes, and you must remember that they form an important part of many birds' diets – so learn to love them!

Around properties, dogs are very numerous, but they are normally fenced in or chained up, and will seldom do more than surprise you.

Attitudes

The Spanish are popularly supposed to be indifferent to the suffering of animals, but this is largely mythical. Exceptions are the keeping of birds as big as Partridges in tiny cages (for use as call-birds), and the well-known one of bull-fighting. The latter, however, is a part of the nation's heritage, and is, at least, responsible for the maintenance of large tracts of open country for the beasts to roam, which are especially good breeding grounds for many rare species of birds. (Though they are potentially dangerous places to wander about in!) In general, the average Spaniard lavishes much care upon his pets, and the increasing awareness of wildlife is heartening.

Access

The problem of access to public and private places is one which exercises the minds of birders everywhere. It is probably less of a problem in Spain than in most European countries – simply because there is more space than in the more overcrowded states of the North.

Everywhere in Spain you will see signs saying, 'Coto privado de caza.' – often shortened to a painted 'Coto' on a wall or bridge. These signs are interspersed with simple squares consisting of black and white triangles. The signs do not mean that you can't go there! They are simply demarcations of hunting rights, establishing exclusivity of jealously-guarded areas for shooting. You should obviously respect the hunters' rights, and avoid disturbing their rabbits and partridges on their favourite winter Sunday mornings.

You may well come across signs, on the other hand, that say 'Prohibido el paso' – this is a clear indication that any incursion will be unwelcome. Other signs may well declare, 'Camino privado' – Private road – and it depends whether you regard this as a deterrent, or a challenge!

Access to working salt-pans is normally totally prohibited, for the best of reasons – they are sensitive places, with carefully-maintained dykes, etc – but you may sometimes obtain access by asking at the appropriate office. Mountain areas seldom have many restrictions, and there are usually enough paths and tracks to enable you to enter areas without disturbing too much of the countryside. As elsewhere, leaving a car by the side of a road can excite the curiosity of locals and police, especially when there has been a recent history of poaching, fire-raising or rustling. Bird-stickers can help to establish your credentials. Chains across paths clearly prevent your vehicular access, but don't mean you can't walk there. As with any part of the world, respect for the privacy of others, and commonsense in general, will dictate. Particular prohibitions concern matters like collecting snails (caracoles), or wild mushrooms (setas) – these should, of course, be respected. In general, however, the Spanish are quite relaxed about access to places where crops and livestock are not to be prejudiced.

Customs and Culture

Although the area we are dealing with is all part of Spain, the first thing that must be realised is that there are, here, four separate 'Comunidades autonomicas.' Spain is split, administratively, into autonomous regions, called 'communities' – each of which comprises one or more Provinces (Andalucia, for example, comprises no less than eight Provinces, whilst others, like Murcia, have only one).

Each community has its own government, federally responsible, of course, to central government in Madrid, but responsible for a wide range of services and possessing a much greater dgree of autonomy than, for example, an English county. A better analogy may well be the US federation of autonomous States. This is all important, as the nation is large, populations having been separated in the days when travel was less easy than today, by some long distances. For this reason, and various historical factors, Spain has a great many cultural differences within its borders, and this is nowhere more obvious than in its linguistic traditions. Hence it is necessary to realise that the limited area covered by this guide encompasses no less than three languages! (Or two, one of which has a dialectic offshoot)

The People

Spanish people are a bit of a mixture. Any country that has had so much turmoil over the centuries will guarantee this, and the Moorish origins of many are easy to see. Moorish roots exist in the language too, and place-names are littered with Arabic constructions – any name beginning with Al . . . for instance, and rivers are often prefixed by Guad..., from the Arabic 'wadi.'

Spanish people have little or no resentment for foreigners, realising that their economy depends in no small part upon tourism. They will help you out of almost any scrape you may find yourself in. They are, of course, proud of their nation, and like to tell you how important is their language, which is, after all, spoken in many countries. It is certainly unwise to enter into political discussions – Franco's days may be the object of nostalgia for some, but their memory will stir bitter hatred in others. The Church still wields some power in the land, but congregations are waning, here as elsewhere.

As in many countries, there is a general distrust of the capital, especially in such fiercely independent places as Cataluña, where a football match between Barcelona and their hated rivals from Madrid will arouse much passion.

Bureaucracy is a major hassle in Spain, with much queueing necessary in a variety of offices, but many Spaniards pay little more than lip-service to it, anyway.

In general then, you will find the average Spaniard extremely outgoing, friendly and helpful, but do try to address him in his own tongue. Even enough words to pass the time of day will be appreciated.

Language

For all practical purposes, the visitor need only learn a few words of Castellano, or standard Iberian Spanish, as this is everywhere understood. But you will see signs with puzzling words in no less than six of the Provinces we address – Catalán in Girona, Barcelona and Tarragona, and Valenciano in Castellón, Valencia and Alicante. Catalán is, in fact, an amalgam of Castellano and French, with a few of its own words thrown in, and some odd-looking spelling habits. Valenciano is nothing more than a dialectic version of Catalán, which has further offshoots in the Balearic Islands. As I say, it is unlikely that you will find anyone unable – or even unwilling – to speak to you in Castellano. You may just, however, find difficulty in some parts, encountering someone who speaks English. This will be no problem, of course, in the major cities, or resorts like Benidorm and Salou, but try asking where you can buy a pair of socks in deepest Teruel, and you may well have to resort to sign-language! Although the Spanish are, in general, not nearly so touchy as the French in this regard, they will still appreciate your efforts to learn their language.

It may be no bad idea to equip youself with, as a minimum, the words for basic foodstuffs, polite greetings, and, possibly, some bird-names. Although Spanish pronunciation rules are always strictly followed – or perhaps because of it – you need to get your pronunciation accurate in order to be understood. Then, of course, the trick is to understand the reply, which often comes in a rapid torrent!

Food & Drink

Like language, food is very regional in Spain. The coast around Valencia is famed for perhaps the best-known Spanish dish outside Spain, the paella. This takes many forms, and the expected sea-food is only one of them. In fact, rabbit and snail paellas are more common in Valencia, whilst the 'paella de marisco' (sea-food) is seen more often in Alicante. Similar are dishes like 'arroz con pollo' – a chicken paella, and arroz con costra, a filling concoction which is basically a paella, with a baked omelette on top. Don't imagine that paella is the only dish typical of Spain! Aragón will give you the opportunity to sample trout, cooked in a variety of ways, roast suckling pig, various stews or barbecued rib of beef. In Albacete, you may well be served Gazpacho Manchego, a rich stew with a type of biscuit soaking up the stock. I have eaten delicious river crayfish there, and the sausages and black-pudding-like 'morcilla' are present in endless variety.

All along the coast, seafood is to be found, of course, and Alicante specialises in 'pescaditos' – literally 'little fish' – as well as a wide variety of shellfish, including supremely sweet clams.

Cataluña also has its specialities, including a tasty whitish sausage 'butifarra' and many seafood dishes.

'Tapas' refers to the plates of food you will see displayed in many bars, often under a glass cover. There may be a huge variety of dishes, and you buy a 'ración' for a few euros or so. The custom arose from the placing (free of charge) of a little plate ('tapa' – or lid) containing a titbit on top of your drink. This is still done in Andalucía, but elsewhere you have to pay for it! Unless you know the bar, it may be wise to avoid mayonnaise-based dishes, like Russian salad, which may be less than fresh!

Restaurants are, in general, obliged to offer a cheap, set, menú, called 'menú del día' every lunchtime, and you will certainly come across some which offer this all evening too. But it is likely that, especially in tourist areas, the set menú will disappear at dinner-time, and you will be forced to order from the much more expensive á la carte menú. Most hotels, however, will be happy to offer you a 'media-pensión' deal, so that you will, in effect, dine from a set menú in the evening.

Wines are produced in many parts of our region, but you will also be offered the classy wines of Rioja, at least in better restaurants. Don't be afraid, however, to try some of the local stuff. Alicante produces some heady, sweetish wines, especially in the Jalon valley, and there are some bigger wine-growing areas in Tarragona Province, in particular.

Beer is drunk everywhere, and is nowadays pretty much of a standard. A shandy is called a 'clara.' Soft drinks are also available, but if you want Diet drinks, you may be restricted to Coca Cola (known as Coca Cola Light, pronounced as in English)

Stronger drink is well represented in Spain, with some excellent – and cheap – brandies, and lots of liqueurs, some of which, like Pacharán, Cantueso and Ponche, are peculiar to the country. Try them!

Coffee is what the Spanish do best, and a 'Café con Leche' is always available at breakfast time. If you want a smaller one, try a 'cortado,' or ask for a 'café solo' – black, or 'Americano' – long and black. Don't ask for a tea with milk, or that is exactly what you'll get – no water! Tea comes with lemon, unless you painstakingly show the man how to do it. You need to be an adict to bother!

Tap water is safe almost anywhere, but bottled water can always be had – just bear in mind that it often causes tummy upsets, or at least, that's what my doctor says.

Meal-times

Breakfast is a rudimentary affair – coffee and toast, or 'madalenas' – buns – or croissants. The Spanish tend, then, to have 'almuerzo' – probably a sandwich, or tapas – at around eleven.

Lunch is a big meal, often at two-thirty to four o'clock.

Dinner is lighter, and may be taken very late – even up to and beyond midnight, especially in summer.

It is likely that visiting birders will prefer not to spend a couple of hours of precious daylight sitting in a restaurant. Excellent bread is easy to find, and the makings of a picnic are not far away.

Fiestas

Spain has more public holidays than any other country in Europe. Besides the ones you will be able to predict, such as Christmas Day, Good Friday and Easter Monday (and the last is not a holiday everywhere!) there are many others, some of which have religious significance, such as All Saints'Day (1st November) and some have political origins, such as Constitution and Labour Days. Then there are the local fiestas. Every town has its own fiesta, usually to commemorate their Patron Saint. This frequently lasts for a week or more, during which all hell breaks loose in the town, and, just in the region we are dealing with, bulls are allowed to run through the streets in more than one town, everyone is pelted with tomatoes in another, whilst others burn painstakingly-constructed papier-maché tableaux. All have massive firework displays, but, in Elche, the tradition is to throw semi-lethal bangers at groups of people in the street! When no more than 83 people were injured, the mayor once came on TV announcing that fact with pride!

So check your calendar before you decide on places to stay – all-night parties may or may not be your 'thing.' Christmas is a low-key affair, with more made of New Year, and the kids receiving their presents on 6th January (Three Kings'). The week leading up to Easter (Semana Santa) is a very big holiday, with all Madrid decamping to the coast or the snows to enjoy the first of the spring sunshine. On Easter Sunday, however, they all clear off back to Madrid, leaving the coast in peace until summer gets under way in early July. Most Spanish people take the whole month of August off, during which time it becomes expensive or impossible to obtain coastal accommodation.

Shopping

Shops in towns are normally open, on weekdays, from nine to two, and five until eight, but major supermarkets outside towns tend to be open from ten until ten, and do not close on Saturday afternoon like the smaller shops. In summer, it is usually possible to find a shop open on Sundays, especially in the morning, and bear in mind that many garages sell (expensive) basic foodstuffs. Local markets are an excellent source of fruit and vegetables, but keep your wallet out of sight!

You may experience difficulty, outside major cities, in finding specialist dealers for optical equipment, etc., and good bookshops are also few and far between.

Pharmacies are announced by a green cross, often illuminated, and they are very clean and well-run, with an array of medicines for all ills. Pharmacists in Spain are highly-qualified, and will be able to treat all but serious problems as well as most doctors. Many medicines available only on prescription in other countries may be bought over the counter.

Medical Care

Should you require medical treatment in Spain, it is essential that you have form E111 with you, unless you are prepared to pay. Even if you are covered by travel insurance, you will almost certainly be asked to pay for the treatment, and recover the cost upon your return. Even small towns usually have clinics, or 'ambulatorios,' where a Social Security doctor can be consulted, and most hospitals will have an emergency centre. Medical care is highly professional, but, as elsewhere, overstretched in terms of resources and time. A translator may well be necessary if you have a serious problem.

Conservation

Spain is, undeniably, behind many Northern European nations in the matter of conservation, but does have a developing strategy. There are few actual National Parks, but many 'Natural Parks' where hunting is prohibited or restricted, and where many public employees and volunteers work hard to provide and maintain the right conditions for wildlife. Spain produces many fine TV natural history flims, which are enjoyed by a lot of people on national channels, ensuring a growing public awareness of conservation issues. To ennumerate the threats to Spain's unique wildlife would only be to repeat what has been written elsewhere, but the principal ones may be summarised thus:–

1. Habitat-loss due to:–
   (a) Residential and industrial development.
   (b) Agriculture, including changes in practice.
   (c) Tourism and leisure.
2. Direct pressure, i.e. hunting.
3. Indirect pressure, due to competition with hunting or agricultural interests.
4. Other threats.

1. (a) Fortunately, Spanish towns do not sprawl in the accepted 'English' way – most people live in high-rise flats, but there is a more recent tendency to live in more rural settings, which may pose a future threat in many areas.

   (b) Changes in agricultural practice have been very prejudicial to species which always got along well with more 'primitive' types of farming, and recent years have seen big declines in sandgrouse, bustards, and Stone Curlew populations, whilst the Corncrake is all but lost. More enlightened land-use, and 'set-aside' systems will be necessary to arrest further declines.

   (c) The ever-increasing demand for holiday-homes, hotels, and leisure facilities, and the insistence of our species on sitting around on sandy beaches, puts immense pressure on shorebirds' habitats, as well as threatening many important coastal wetlands and woodlands.
2. Hunting is a big menace in Spain. Although the taking of most species you will think of as 'important' is prohibited by law, those responsible for enforcement are too few, and have too few powers, to prevent much furtive hunting. The residual menace of lead-shot,

FRANCE

PAIS VASCO

NAVARRA

ANDORRA

GIRONA

Girona

LERIDA

CATALONIA

LA RIOJA

Huesca

ARAGON

BARCELONA

Barcelona

CASTILLA Y LEON

Zaragoza

Lérida

Tarragona

TARRAGONA

Tortosa

TERUEL

Teruel

CASTELLON

Mediterranean Sea

Palma

CUENCA

Cuenca

CASTILLA - LA MANCHA

Valencia

VALENCIA

BALEARICS

VALENCIA

Albacete

ALBACETE

ALICANTE

Alicante

MURCIA

ANDALUCIA

—··—··—	International Bdy
– – – – –	Regional Bdy
················	Provincial Bdy
————	Motorways
————	Other roads
● ■	Towns/Cities

SPAIN

Girona
Barcelona
Tarragona
Teruel
Castellón
Cuenca
Valencia
Albacete
Alicante

subsequently ingested by water-birds, poses a serious threat to many species, particularly Flamingo. There remain one or two anomalies amongst the species which do not enjoy protection – Garganey comes to mind here – and legislation is in need of revision. There is always the further concern that hunters may not be sufficiently proficient to identify the species they may – or may not – take.

3. Poisoning of birds of prey still takes place, though efforts are continually made to stop the practice.

4. Power-lines present a problem for night-flying birds, and some authorities have now responded by 'decorating' the lines with coloured tags.

The roads are another hazard, and important numbers of birds are killed annually by traffic.

Perhaps the answer to all these problems lies in education. Not only do the young require this – the older hunters are probably a 'lost cause' – but the authorities too need persuading that the future lies in providing for 'green tourism.' Enough people need to write to the various tourist offices for anyone to take notice. There is, in fact, an increasing number of interested and committed young people in Spain, but the country lacks any body like the RSPB, whose massive membership forms an important lobby in Britain.

Perhaps, ultimately, it will require an entrepreneurial approach, with someone providing observation/information/sales centres as a business venture, before the various local governments will awaken to the tremendous opportunities that their wildlife sites present.

The Area Covered by this Guide

We must begin by saying that no guide can cover all of eastern Spain, and it is necessary to read this work in conjunction with the 'Birdwatching Guide to the Pyrenees,' and the 'Birdwatching Guide to Southern Spain,' both published by Arlequin Press, with which it is meant to be complementary.

In general, the area covered may be defined as follows:–

The whole of the coastal strip, from the French frontier down to the southern boundary of the Province of Alicante (the northern end of the Mar Menor), and those sites within a comfortable day-trip-range inland, except where they are covered by the Pyrenees guide.

The guide therefore confines itself, in Cataluña, to the coastal strip, whereas further south, it extends to cover the whole of the Valencian Community, and adjacent areas, which encroach on Teruel Province (Aragón) and Albacete and Cuenca (Castilla-la Mancha).

It may therefore be of use to anyone holidaying at coastal resorts served by, particularly, the airports of Reus, Valencia and Alicante, or those who may be touring the eastern part of Spain, possibly in conjunction with other regions.

Politically, the greater part of this guide is concentrated upon the autonomous region of Valencia, where the majority of the sites are to be found, but the hugely important Ebro Delta, as well as other important coastal marshes further north, lie within the Region of Cataluña. A separate chapter touches upon the cultural and linguistic disparities which exist within this fascinating area, and it is hoped that the visitor will spend enough time here to enjoy not only the birdlife, but the rich heritage and superb scenery which lie within it.

For the sake of tidiness, we treat sites covered by this guide broadly under Provincial headings, although there are cases where sites straddle boundaries. The Provincial summaries are followed by lists of sites covered. The order in which the Provinces are to be found in this guide follows a more-or-less logical north-south sequence.

If it is apparent that the guide favours Alicante Province, and the south of the region in general, we make no apology, as we feel that a) This part of the coast offers the greatest bio-diversity, and therefore the best selection of bird-species, and b) (possibly more important) the majority of users of this guide will be likely to select Alicante Province as the base for their holidays. This is by no means to denigrate the claims of such wonderful places as the Ebro Delta and Gallocanta, but they are just that much more inaccessible to most.

Further Afield

As mentioned in the chapter on 'The Area Covered by this Guide' the Arlequin Press publications cover adjacent areas to the north and south, respectively, of our region, and some of the places covered in those guides are within relatively easy reach of centres where users of the present volume may stay. In particular, the visitor to the coast of Cataluña may well like to combine a birding holiday there with a visit to the Pyrenees, and also take a look at the plains of Belchite, and other sites in Zaragoza Province. Those staying around Alicante, on the other hand, will find the Murcia sites described in the 'Southern Spain' volume, readily accessible.

For the more adventurous soul, practically the whole of central Spain is within a day's drive of the east coast, and offers many exciting prospects. Take, for instance, a weekend trip to the great valley of Los Cabañeros, northwest of Ciudad Real, where Black-shouldered Kite and Imperial Eagle, Azure-winged Magpie and Black Vulture are found. Or visit the fabulous Tablas de Daimiel for its superb wetland habitats. Try the lagoons of Castilla-la Mancha, where water birds and steppe species are found side-by-side, or the mountains of the Sierra de Cazorla, where raptors are plentiful – the list is endless. Spain is a country of great contrasts, sparse human population, and terrific variety.

Diversions

All birders do not necessarily want to spend their entire holiday birding (this will be heresy to some!) and there may well be other members of the family to consider. Aside from the fiestas already mentioned in these pages, there are many other sights to delight the eyes in this region of Spain. Traditional holiday entertainments such as sunning oneself on the beach can here be augmented by visits to spectacular castles, such as the famous one at Guadalest, near Benidorm, and the less publicised but equally impressive ones at Castalla, Sax and Villena, for instance. Further north, the beauty of the Maestrazgo region, to the north of Castellón Province, is worth a look, and there is a wonderful fortified town at Morella. Other superb old villages and towns are too numerous to mention, but a particular favourite of mine is the ancient town of Alberracín, to the west of Teruel.

Fine sophisticated cities, with excellent shopping, are found throughout the region, and Valencia even has a Marks and Spencers! Barcelona would require a guide on its own, of course, but has a multiplicity of attractions, ranging from Gaudi's almost unreal cathedral, to the possibility of seeing a football match at Europe's greatest stadium, the Nou Camp.

Alicante has a fine castle, and a sophisticated modern marina, and most of the other towns, especially the Provincial capitals, have older parts which would repay a visit.

For those with more modern tastes, and particularly those with children, the new Port Aventura is a major theme park, near Salou, whilst another is currently being built near Benidorm, which has a wealth of entertainment to suit all tastes. Bullfights can be seen in most towns, if you happen upon them during a fiesta, and sporting opportunities include many fine golf courses.

You need never be bored in Eastern Spain!

Alicante

A whole book can be devoted to this highly complex Province, which is one of Spain's most important ones ornithologically, both for the extent and diversity of its breeding populations, and for the sites it offers wintering and migrating birds.

The north of the Province is ruggedly and scenically mountainous, with some sharp and impressive peaks, the occasional high plateau, and some verdant valleys. The south is mainly agricultural plain, with wetlands of huge importance, but also some low hills, clothed in pinewoods, and more rocky mountain ranges. Much of the coast is a succession of ribbon resort-development, but odd rocky headlands and islands are of some interest. Communications are characterised by the A7 motorway, which runs right through the Province, and the N330 highway from Alicante to Madrid, which means that the Province is easily accessible by road. The airport at El Altet serves Alicante with regular and charter flights from all over Europe, and there are sea connections between Alicante and Oran, Algeria, and Denia and Ibiza.

Alicante Sites
A1: The Northern Sierras.
A2: The Cabo de la Nao, and other coastal sites.
A3: Sierra de Santa Pola, and Clot de Galvany.
A4: Tabarca.
A5: Salinas de Santa Pola.
A6: El Hondo de Elche.
A7: The Mouth of the Segura.
A8: La Mata.
A9: Embalse de la Pedrera.
A10: Sierra de Salinas.

Site A1. THE NORTHERN SIERRAS

This is scarcely to be regarded as a single site, but it is a relatively small area of mountainous country, and can be searched quite thoroughly in a couple of days. Not particularly
rich in raptors, there are, however, several pairs of Bonelli's Eagles, at least three pairs of
Golden Eagles, and a few pairs of Peregrine. Lesser Kestrel are possible. The whole area
is criss-crossed by winding roads, and is largely accessible at any time of the year, but
much the best time to visit is in spring. A summer trip from the coast however, may provide
a welcome relief from the heat. It is best to treat the region in terms of 'sub-sites,' but this
certainly doesn't mean that there are no other spots which could turn up good birds – the
whole area merits extensive exploration.

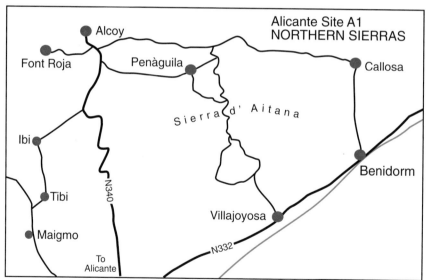

(a) Aitana
Patches of woodland around the 'Safari Park' can be good for tits, breeding Woodlark,
Bonelli's Warbler, Jay, Cirl Bunting and Mistle Thrush, whilst on the higher plateau, around
the radar station, Rock Sparrow, Chough, Rock Bunting and Rock Thrush are often seen.

(b) Penáguila
The spectacular ravine just outside the town (you will recognise it from the hole in the rock
at the top), has breeding Bonelli's Eagle in some years, and always sports a Rock Sparrow

20

Woodlark

colony in summer. Blue Rock Thrush, Chough and Black Redstart are regular here too. The deep valley between here and Gorga has a fine stand of poplars, and is reliable for Golden Oriole, Spotted Flycatcher and probably Melodious Warbler.

(c) The Font Roja
Take the signposted road from just south of Alcoy, and proceed to the hermitage at the top. Here you can walk in beautiful scenery, and gain good views of all the woodland birds, including Short-toed Treecreeper, Crested Tit, and Cirl Bunting. There are also breeding Goshawk, Sparrowhawk, Eagle Owl, Bonelli's Eagle, Orphean Warbler and Subalpine Warbler here, and mammals include Wild Boar and Wild Cat.

(d) Maigmó
The narrow road which leads off the A213 provides an opportunity to see some of the typical birds of the zone, in a brief excursion from Alicante. Crossbills abound here, and frequently come to drink at some little artificial pools in the garden of a children's nature centre to the left of the road. Crested Tit, Rock Bunting and Woodlark are common, and a pair of Golden Eagle are quite often seen here.

The whole area is one of spectacular, sunlit mountains, and you can find birds almost anywhere, but you may well have to work for them. Red-rumped Swallow is a species which seems to crop up in different spots every year (though a regular pair breeds in the dam of the reservoir at Tibi), and there is also a chance of finding a Great Spotted Cuckoo, wherever you come across Magpies.

Practical Points
Hotels and restaurants are plentiful on the coast, of course, and Alcoy also has a lot to offer, being a surprisingly large, busy town. Allow plenty of time for the mountain roads, though most are usually in good condition. Guadalest is something of a tourist 'mecca' – and may be best avoided, although there may be dissent from some members of your party!

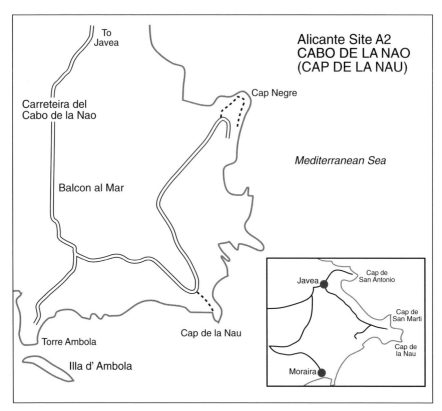

Site A2. CABO DE LA NAO AND OTHER COASTAL SITES

This site lies at the eastern extremity of the Alicante coast, and you can actually see Ibiza on a clear day from these parts! The Cabo de San Antonio is some little way to the north, and the Cabo de San Martin lies between the two. All can be good for sea-watching, and spring and autumn migrants can turn up almost anywhere. You can usefully combine the visit with a look at the redundant saltpans at Calpe, where Audouin's Gulls are reliable, or, if you are more energetically-inclined, a climb up the Peñon de Ifach, where Peregrine are usually about. Both species of common shearwater pass along this coast at migration times, and numbers, particularly of Mediterranean Shearwater, can be spectacular. Skuas, Gannet, and terns are regular, of course. Pallid Swift, Thekla Lark and Spectacled Warbler breed on the headlands, and the scrub can be excellent for migrant warblers when there is any movement. Blue Rock Thrush and Black Wheatear breed commonly. Pines in the area hold many Crested Tits and Short-toed Treecreepers, with Siskin as a frequent visitor outside the nesting season. There have been recent winter records of Red-breasted Flycatcher in this area.

The maps show the best points of access.

Practical Points

This is a very busy area in peak holiday periods, but accommodation should pose little problem outside July and August.

It should not need to be said that care should be exercised when negotiating cliff-top paths!

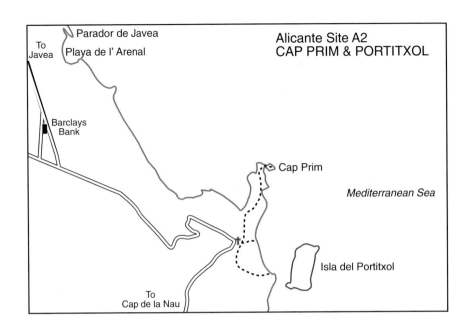

Alicante Site A2
CAP PRIM & PORTITXOL

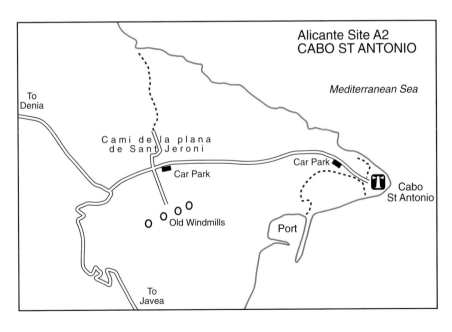

Alicante Site A2
CABO ST ANTONIO

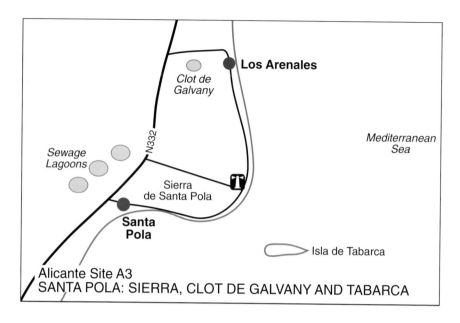

Alicante Site A3
SANTA POLA: SIERRA, CLOT DE GALVANY AND TABARCA

Site A3. SIERRA DE SANTA POLA & CLOT DE GALVANY

The Sierra de Santa Pola is something of a euphemism for a low rocky hill, separating Santa Pola from the urbanisations of Gran Alacant to the north, and culminating in the headland, or Cabo de Santa Pola, which looks out over Tabarca (q.v.). It is relatively undisturbed (for the moment, at least) and does not suffer from a great deal of human activity, although the greater part of the plateau is, in fact, planted with pines. To the west of the N332 coastal road lies the 'Depuradora' or sewage lagoon complex.

The Clot de Galvany is a small wetland, sandwiched between the coast road and some sprawling new urbanisations, although it does enjoy a limited reserve status. The two sites are sufficiently close together to be treated under one heading, though they are different in character.

The great interest in terms of breeding birds on the Sierra is the presence of two species which tend to be on most northern Europeans' list of wanted birds: Red-necked Nightjar and Rufous Bush Robin. The former is easy enough, if you go to the area just south of the lighthouse road at dusk (no earlier!) in late April to late July. You will often pick one up in the headlights if you take the track down into Santa Pola later. The latter is tougher. Search the pine plantations during May/June, and listen for the 'Robin-with-a-sore-throat' song. Patience will be rewarded (there are some 10-20 pairs at least, in most years). Stone Curlew, Black-eared Wheatear, Woodchat Shrike, Thekla and Short-toed Lark, and, oddly, Common Nightjar, also breed. At passage times, the hillsides can come alive with warblers and flycatchers, and the wires along the lighthouse road are a good bet for shrikes, Roller, and the like. The cliffs hold Black Wheatear and Blue Rock Thrush. The sewage lagoons are always worth a look, but what you see will depend upon water-levels. Ruddy Shelduck has been fairly regular in recent years, and all the marsh terns, as well as a variety of waders, are likely. Passage raptors favour the area, especially on westerly winds.

The Clot de Galvany, though small, is of considerable interest. Both Ferruginous and Marbled Duck have bred in recent times, and Glossy Ibis has been seen, whilst the reeds are worth checking for warblers. If the marsh to the east is flooded, as in many springs, it can be very good for passage waders.

There is a new hide set up to overlook a small pond at the coastal end of the Clot, which should be worth a visit.

Practical Points
Some of the tracks in the area are rather stony, and require care, especially if driving at night. Mosquitoes can be a bit troublesome here, particularly on spring evenings, so it pays to wear more clothes than the climate may suggest. Caution should be exercised around the precipitous cliffs which surround the lighthouse.

There are a few hotels in Santa Pola, and the Polamar, in particular, comes well-recommended. The town has an ample supply of restaurants and bars.

Site A4. TABARCA
Tabarca is a small island some 4 kilometres off Santa Pola, and reachable by boat from that port, as well as from Alicante, and, in summer, from Torrevieja. The journey from Santa Pola takes about half an hour, and is quite pleasant, with always a chance of a few Mediterranean Shearwaters, and the near-certainty of Audouin's Gull, on the crossing. Once you arrive on the island – and you will usually want to get the earliest boat, at ten o'clock, it pays to make for the prickly-pear entanglement near to the prominent old tower, to the southeast of the landing. Here, you will soon know if there are migrants to be found, as this area can heave with birds if there has been an arrival. Further east is a wild area of scrub and low vegetation, which can be worth searching for Wheatears, Quail and the like. May and September are probably the best months, and the variety of warblers can be excellent, but it can also be fairly quiet, when you will have to content yourself by looking at the few breeding species – Thekla Lark and Pallid Swift are perhaps the 'best,' though Storm Petrel and possibly Audouin's Gull nest sparingly on the offshore rocks.

Practical Points
There is an hotel on the island, the 'Casa del Gobernador' and innumerable restaurants, to feed the huge number of day-trippers who come across in summer to swim, sunbathe and feed on the excellent fish. The crossing can be surprisingly rough when the sea-breeze gets up in the afternoon. A hat is probably essential, and a bottle of water very useful, as it can get extremely hot here. Anyone interested in snorkelling will find plenty to pass a few idle hours.

Short-toed Lark

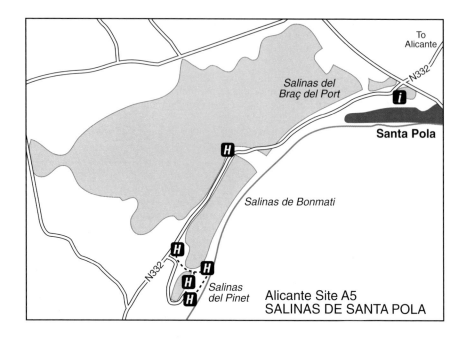

Site A5. SANTA POLA SALINAS

One of the most important sites on the Mediterranean coast of Spain, the Salinas of Santa Pola cannot be mentioned without bringing El Hondo into the equation, as they really form one major wetland, of interest at all seasons of the year. The N332 road forms a dreadful nuisance to birders wishing to investigate this wonderful place, and it is along this road that we must travel, looking at the first available lagoons that you approach from the north. Taking the slip-road to the right, you come to the traffic-lights under the road you have just left. Here you can park at the back of the inn on the right, and look over a shallow lagoon, for your first view of the typical Avocets, Flamingo and other wading birds. Over on the other (Santa Pola) side of the road, a small reserve has been created, where some injured Flamingo are allowed to rest on islands specially created. There are Red-crested Pochard and egrets here too, and a nice variety of waders usually includes Greenshank and Spotted Redshank. Moving on along the N332, you can leave it immediately after you pass the horrific funfair on the left, turning right on a rough road. From some way along this, take a branch-track to the left, and park to look out across working saltpans. You should find Audouin's Gull here, especially in late summer, and other gulls are always about, as well as waders. The area is good in winter for Bluethroat and Penduline Tit.

Carrying on across the salinas, you can stop near the old, ruined tower, and again a little further on, for good views over the vast lakes. Here you can get lots of grebes and duck, large Flamingo flocks, herons, and waders.

Stop a little further on, near the entrance to the Bonmati saltworks, for Slender-billed Gull, Osprey and more waders, then carry on to turn left just beyond the petrol station, and take a winding road to El Pinet, where you can get away from the traffic and look across the same salinas in peace. This is a good spot for terns, especially Sandwich, Audouin's and Mediterranean Gulls, and a variety of migrants. A look at the sea in this area may reveal feeding rafts of Mediterranean Shearwaters in the bay.

Inland, it is difficult to get to good birding at the 'back' of the salinas, but there are tracks taking you along close to the edge of the reeds, particularly in the vicinity of 'Casa Irles' – a good spot for the odd small party of Cranes in winter, and reliable area for Marsh Harrier. Glossy Ibis have bred in this part recently.

Practical Points

The N332 road is a racetrack, and any manoeuvres should be carried out with great care. Santa Pola and La Marina have hotels and restaurants, the Polamar and Patilla in Santa Pola both being comfortable hotels. The 'Gran Via' restaurant in La Marina is famous for its rice-dishes. There are also plenty of places to rent on a holiday basis, and Santa Pola makes a fine base for a family holiday, with beaches as good as anywhere.

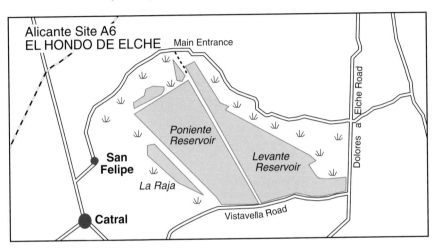

Site A6. EL HONDO DE ELCHE

El Hondo is a reservoir, or rather a pair of reservoirs, set in low-lying land, directly inland from the Salinas de Santa Pola (q.v.) The two reservoirs, the eastern 'Levante' (450 hectares) and the western 'Poniente' (650 hectares) are surrounded by extensive reedbeds, and numerous smaller lagoons and pools, a few of which have permanent water. Originally, they formed, with the Salinas de Santa Pola, the 'Albufera de Elche.'

The whole is used as an irrigation reservoir, and, though efforts are naturally made to control water-levels, there is a grave tendency for the whole lot to dry out completely in drought-years, which occur not infrequently. Hunting, both officially-controlled and furtive, is a problem for the whole area, particularly as a result of the resultant excessive quantities of lead-shot thereby deposited, which poses a real threat to the Flamingo population, and other bottom-feeding birds.

At this moment, El Hondo is probably the best place in Europe to see two species, Namely White-headed and Marbled Ducks.

There are various sites scattered around the periphery of the reserve where you can observe a great variety of species without entry into the reserve itself, but access can be arranged, by telephoning in advance, to 96-667-85-15, and arranging to be met at the main entrance.

Peripheral sites which should be part of any birder's itinerary, should be the Vistavella road, and views over the southern ponds, the ponds of La Raja, and, a little further away, the fishponds of El Hondo de Amoros, reliable at any season. Palm-groves, at the northern boundary of the reserve, and especially the semi-abandoned ones, are worth a look, especially in summer, as Wryneck, Roller and Short-toed Treecreeper have all recently bred.

To list the birds of El Hondo would require a book in itself, but a seasonal listing of the most significant and characteristic species is in order:-

Winter
Black-necked Grebe, herons, including the occasional wintering Squacco and Little Bittern, duck, including White-headed, and huge flocks of Shoveler, Pintail, etc. Raptors, of a good variety, including Booted and sometimes Spotted Eagle, Hen and Marsh Harrier (with a notable roost), Sparrowhawk, Merlin, Peregrine. Rails and crakes, including, Purple Gallinule, Cranes (in surrounding fields) waders including Ruff, Wood and Green Sandpiper, Kingfisher, Bluethroat, Penduline Tit, Moustached Warbler, millions of Chiffchaff, and always the possibility of a major rarity.

Spring and autumn
Spectacular hirundine and swift passage, terns, waders, arriving herons, and passing raptors.

Breeding
Flamingo, herons, including Night, Purple and Grey Herons, and Little Bittern. Whiskered Tern, Marbled and White-headed Duck, Montagu's Harrier, Great Reed Warbler, Collared Pratincole.

Put simply, El Hondo is a 'must' and the species list above is no more than a brief outline – you can comfortably log up 50 or 60 species in a morning in spring or autumn, and the unexpected is definitely to be expected here!

Practical Points
Accomodation is readily available in Santa Pola, and there is a Parador in Elche, for those of more sophisticated bent.

Purple Heron

Camping sites are scattered freely along the coast.

Some of the roads around El Hondo are heavily pot-holed, and should be driven with care. In common with all marshy areas, mosquitoes can be a nuisance, especially if it is still. It is advisable to have a drink with you in summer, as bars can be quite distant, and it is a shame if you gain access, only to have to depart early for a 'rehydrating-session.'

Two restaurants worthy of note are the Venta Ursula, on the Elche-Dolores road, and Casa Hari, at San Felipe Neri, near Catral which specialises in game.

Site A7. The Rio Segura
This is one of the longer rivers in southern Spain, but is nothing more than a polluted trickle, except after heavy rains, where it flows out to the sea, near Guardamar. It is contained between man-made stone walls throughout this stretch, and these walls are topped by tracks, which make convenient viewing points for the birds, which feed and nest in the luxuriant vegetation which grows along the watercourse. Work is constantly being carried out to develop roads in this area, and it changes from year to year, but the seaward side of the bridge at Guardamar is saline, and subject to the slight Mediterranean tides. It is good for resting terns, gulls and salt-water waders, and is frequently visited by Ospreys.

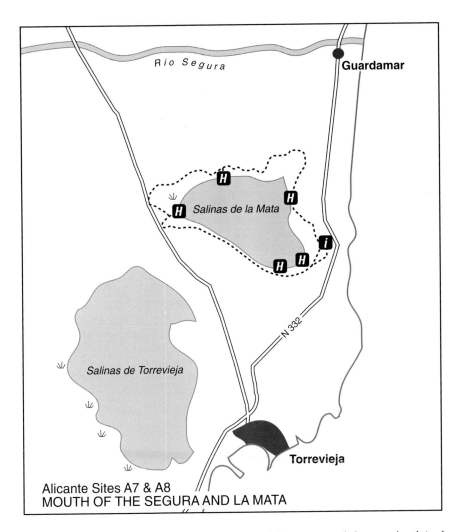

Alicante Sites A7 & A8
MOUTH OF THE SEGURA AND LA MATA

Inland, the vegetation often hold migrants at the right season, and the occasional (and seasonal) freshwater pool may be worth checking for waders, such as Snipe in winter, Temminck's Stint and Marsh Sandpiper in spring. Bluethroat are common in winter, and Olivaceous Warbler breed in the area. The eucalyptus plantation near the river mouth can heave with migrants, and is a good spot for a Golden Oriole, as well as flycatchers and warblers. Raptors often follow the river inland.

Practical Points
Although some of the riverside tracks are designated 'private,' this does not seem to be taken too seriously. However, you should take care not to obstruct the roadway, especially if lorries are using it. Accomodation nearby takes the form of a new hotel and campsite, just off the N332 road a kilometre or so to the north, and several others in Guardamar. If you are tempted to leave your car in the dunes (picnic area), just south of the rivermouth, note that theft from cars is commonplace here.

29

Site A8. LA MATA/TORREVIEJA

La Mata is a big saline lake, extending to 700 hectares, just inland of the N332 road, a short way north of the busy resort of Torrevieja. It has been declared a Nature Reserve, with an Interpretation Centre, hides and trails – a valiant effort, and one which is already bearing fruit. The better end of the lake is the seaward, eastern end, where a hide (best in the mornings) overlooks a big area of mud, excellent for waders, Audouin's and Slender-billed Gull.

La Mata's coastal position means that the bird populations are constantly changing, with a lot of visible migration through the reserve. Breeding species are limited, but more may do so as conservation measures are improved. The real value of the reserve is for wintering Black-necked Grebe, which may number as many as 3,000, and the Stone Curlew flock, at the same season, which can reach an impressive 300 or so. Audouin's Gulls roost at all seasons. Check out the woodland to the left (south) of the hide already mentioned, for migrant songbirds, and the little reedbed at the western end for harriers. More wader-habitat is found here too, and there is an (evening-oriented) hide.

Torrevieja salt-lake is a working, salt-producing environment, whose waters are too salty for birds, but the surrounding reedbeds hold important breeding populations of Montagu's Harrier, and roosting areas for gulls are also worth a mention.

Practical Points

A telescope is essential here, and heat-haze can be a problem. Torrevieja is a thriving resort, but has few hotels – it may be best to use Guardamar as a centre.

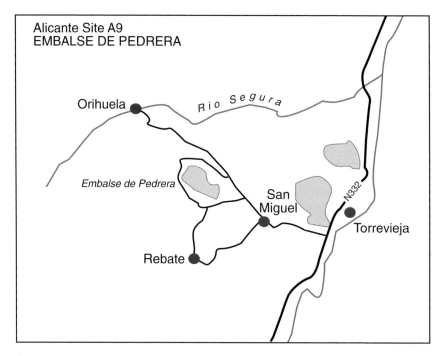

Alicante Site A9
EMBALSE DE PEDRERA

Site A9. EMBALSE DE PEDRERA, AND THE SIERRA DE ESCALONA

This site, or collection of sites, consists of a drinking-water reservoir, only moderately interesting in itself, and the surrounding, barren landscape, together with more fertile, cultivated, areas nearby.

Red-rumped Swallow have bred in the reservoir installations in recent years, and are regular in this area, which is also good for Bee Eaters and larks. The stony fields near the reservoir are worth scanning for Stone Curlew, whilst shrikes and other insectivorous birds are numerous.

The Sierra is known as a post-breeding dispersal area for raptors, particularly the smaller eagles.

From the San Miguel-Rebate road, on summer evenings, you can usually be sure of hearing Red-necked Nightjar, even if you don't see them! A little further afield, the roads down to the coast, both from Rebate, and from San Miguel, go through quiet country of wooded hillsides, where raptors are frequent. Eagle Owl breed in the area, and the huge municipal tip along the road from San Miguel to Campoamor exercises an attraction for raptors, as well as big flocks of gulls, Cattle Egrets and Jackdaws.

Practical Points

There is a campsite at San Miguel, and several others around Torrevieja. there is no shortage of hotels and restaurants in the general area, but little human habitation in the immediate vicinity of the reservoir. The road around the shallow eastern end of the water is rough but easily driveable.

If you do a nocturnal sortie along the Rebate road, do not be surprised if you are interviewed by the security forces, as arsonists and other ne'er-do-wells have apparently been caught in this area in the past. Show your binoculars to them, and they'll go away, shaking their heads.

Orihuela, nearby, is a fascinating, historic city.

Site A10. SIERRA DE SALINAS

A large, quite unfrequented area, this, and one which merits further study. The north-western slopes of the range are best approached from the Villena-Pinoso road, which you leave, on an (initially) excellent road, turning to the left at km.13. This road often gives views of raptors, amongst which you should see, in summer, Short-toed and Booted Eagles. It winds upwards, and deteriorates, but is always reasonable. You can leave your car and walk at several points, when you should find all the usual high-country species, including tits, Short-toed Treecreeper, Rock Bunting and Crossbill, as well as Subalpine, Dartford and probably Orphean Warbler. It is a good area for snakes and lizards, and the views you will get over country to the north and west are stunning. (Incidentally, the road from Yecla to Jumilla is a winter site for Great Bustard in many years). The road eventually winds downhill to rejoin the Pinoso road.

Moving around to the opposite side of the Sierra, the village of Salinas is as good a starting-point as any. The salt-lake is usually bone-dry these days, but can hold excellent bird populations if there is any water. Otherwise, Short-toed Lark is about the sole interesting species hereabouts.

A road winds up, however, from the back of the village, to the Casa del Tío Vidal, from where you can climb higher on foot, or simply 'scope towards the obvious crags. Here you may well find Bonelli's Eagle and Peregrine, as well as plenty of smaller birds. Chough and Rock Sparrow are found as well. You can also follow the Sierra along its southwestern edge, on a narrow road towards Villena (not shown on the Michelin maps), and gain good views of the higher points. The cultivated areas here can also be worth a look, particularly at passage times.

Between Villena and las Virtudes is an area of old salt-pans, where Black-bellied Sandgrouse are occasionally seen, especially in winter. More typically, you will see Lesser Short-toed Lark and Stone Curlew in the area.

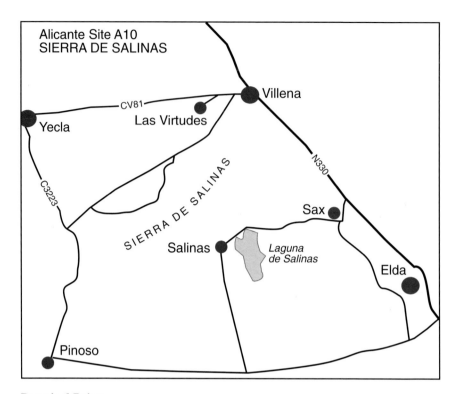

Alicante Site A10
SIERRA DE SALINAS

Villena
CV81
Yecla
Las Virtudes
C3223
SIERRA DE SALINAS
N330
Sax
Salinas
Laguna
de Salinas
Elda
Pinoso

Practical Points
The road along the northwestern ridge requires a reasonably good nerve, and many of those mentioned in this area are narrow, as well as having indifferent surfaces. Accommodation for visiting this area is to be found in the shape of various hostals, both in Villena and along the main N430 towards Madrid. As with all sites in this region, midday temperatures can soar uncomfortably in midsummer, and it can be surprisingly cold on a windy winter's day.

Plate 1. Cabo de Creus (Cap de Creus), Girona.

Plate 2. Delta del Ebro, Tarragona.

Plate 3. Delta del Ebro.

Plate 4. Maestrazgo region, Castellón.

Plate 5. Albufera de Valencia.

Plate 6. Albufera.

Plate 7. Laguna de Pétrola, Albacete.

Plate 8. Marjal de Pego, Valencia/Alicante.

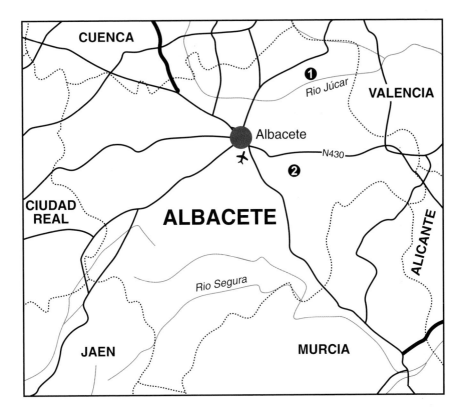

Albacete

As with Cuenca, the western part of this part of the huge Community of Castilla-la Mancha lies outside the scope of this guide. The enormous cereal fields of the eastern part, however, give us the opportunity to look at a habitat not found in the busy coastal regions, and to look for species more normally sought in the plains of west-central Spain. Practically the whole of Albacete is given over to prairie-farming of this type, but here and there shallow lagoons break up the landscape, shimmering with heat-haze under the merciless summer sun, and bleak and sharp with the frosts of winter, because most of this land lies at more than 700 metres above sea-level. there is little human population – just what is necessary to maintain the agricultural business of the region. the road from Alicante to Madrid passes, as straight as an arrow, through the area, and this can be fiendishly busy on summer and Easter weekends, as the Madrileños make their way to and from the coast. Most of the towns are simply agricultural communities, but the road brings with it the usual crop of motels and other facilities.

Albacete Sites
AB1. Alcalá del Júcar.
AB2. Pétrola and area.

Rock Sparrow

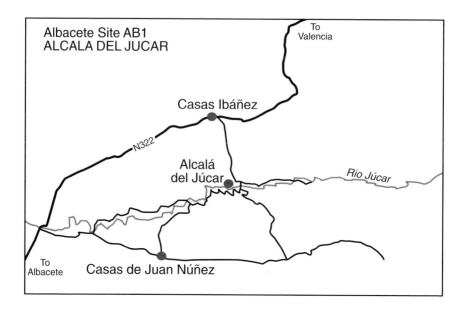

Albacete Site AB1
ALCALA DEL JUCAR

To Valencia

Casas Ibáñez

N322

Alcalá del Júcar

Rio Júcar

To Albacete

Casas de Juan Núñez

Site AB1. ALCALÁ DEL JÚCAR

This is merely a convenient spot to make a base for exploring the Hoz del Júcar, or the gorge of the river of that name. Alcalá is a touristy sort of little town, nestling in the bottom of a spectacular gorge, which comes upon you all of a sudden, especially if you approach it from the north, on the road from Casas Ibañez. The gorge, is, in fact, set in quite unspectacular country, with wide agricultural plains stretching away to the horizon wherever you look.

Once down in the depths, between the limestone cliffs, you are in a different world. The verdant river valley supports breeding species like Melodious and Cetti's Warblers, Wryneck, Nightingale, Great Spotted Woodpecker and Golden Oriole, whilst the cliffs are home to an unusually large population of Rock Sparrow, together with Rock Dove, Black Wheatear, Blue Rock Thrush and colonies of Alpine Swift. In the winter, many Buzzards are to be found in this area, and breeding raptors include Peregrine and Eagle Owl. On passage, large numbers of birds tend to show up in these types of valley, including flycatchers and warblers. Ring Ouzels are characteristic birds on autumn passage. The fields above the gorge, especially the plains to the south, are rich in Stone Curlew and Little Bustard occur. Bee Eaters frequently hawk along the cliff-edges, joined at passage times by huge numbers of hirundines.

Practical Points

There is a range of hotels in Alcalá, as well as many restaurants and bars. It should be borne in mind that the heat can be intense here in summer, as little breeze penetrates into the valley. In winter, the cold can be equally intense, especially on the bleak plains above. Birders will find winter daylight much reduced by the location within the steep walls of the gorge. The valley-bottom roads are narrow and winding, but there are normally ample places to park.

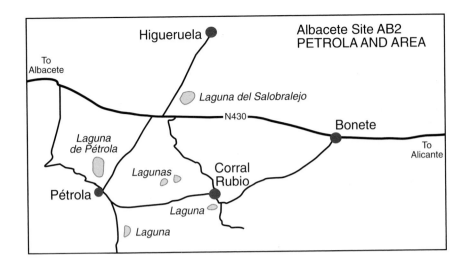

Site AB2. PÉTROLA AND AREA

This is a major site (or aggregation of several sites) which merits a good deal of exploration and time spent. It is an area of undulating plains, largely given over to cereal cultivation, but with small patches 'set aside,' a fair number of shallow, seasonal lagoons, and at least three more-or-less permanent stretches of water. these vary widely from year to year, depending on the winter precipitation.

Although some way to the north of the main areas, the lagoon of Salobralejo is normally the first spot on the itinerary, as you can actually see it from the main N430 road, which you leave, turning briefly to the north, for Higueruela. Almost immediately, a goodish track strikes off to the right, and you go alongside the railway on this. Stopping near farm buildings, you can 'scope across to the lagoon, which always looks worthy of a better investigation – and seldom yields anything of note!

Back under the motorway, you head for Pétrola, and can do a detour to the right just past a prominent ranch. The track is negotiable in a car, with care, and, from a line of pines, you can scan the fields, across to a small lagoon, which has breeding Avocets and Whiskered Terns in good years. Great Spotted Cuckoo are frequent here, with plenty of Magpies to parasitise.

The Pétrola lagoon is the next place to look at, and it can be very good indeed. Gull-billed Tern, Shelduck, white-headed duck, Lapwing and Black-winged Stilts are amongst the breeding species, and raptors usually show up, often including Peregrine and Marsh Harrier. In winter, it is an important site for duck of many species. A track can be found which goes right around the lake, with plenty of spots from which to view it in any light-conditions.

Passage waders are often good here, and Flamingo are currently starting to breed, 100 young in 2000.

Leaving Pétrola for Fuente Alamo, pass the crossroads atop the rise outside town, and take an immediate left down an unsurfaced but wide and fairly flat agricultural road, out across the plains. After perhaps three hundred metres, take a right-angle turn right, and go back, almost towards the Fuente Alamo road (from which you can also view the area, though less well).

Stop near a small stone shed, and you have a great view across rolling plains, and over – most years – a patch of shallow water. In this area, you only really require patience to get

39

a look at Great Bustard, unless agricultural activity has temporarily moved them away. The farming people hereabouts, are, however, quite helpful, and will usually suggest where you may see these most recognisable of birds. Pin-tailed Sandgrouse should also be seen. The water often holds good populations of Red-crested Pochard, and raptors are frequent. Calandra Larks are common, especially in spring, but a good time to see the bustards is immediately after the harvest, in late July.

Although there are huge numbers, and many kilometres, of tracks to be explored, you may then wish to head for Corral Rubio, just outside which village is an excellent lagoon, with breeding marsh terns, a good chance of Pratincoles, many waders, and a variety of wintering wildfowl.

The villages may well have Rock Sparrow around the buildings and stony ground.

Practical Points

This is an area at close to 3,000 feet above sea-level, and has a harsh climate, with a tendency to be bitterly cold in winter, and baking in summer, when the heat-haze can pose a real problem after mid-morning. Be prepared to put your car through a carwash after a few hours on the dusty tracks, and avoid obstructing the farm vehicles.

There are numerous hostelries dotted along the N430, and Albacete city, only a half-hour distant, offers a good range of hotels and restaurants.

The region is noted for its handicrafts – particularly knives – and has many traditional dishes, particularly the filling Gazpacho Manchego.

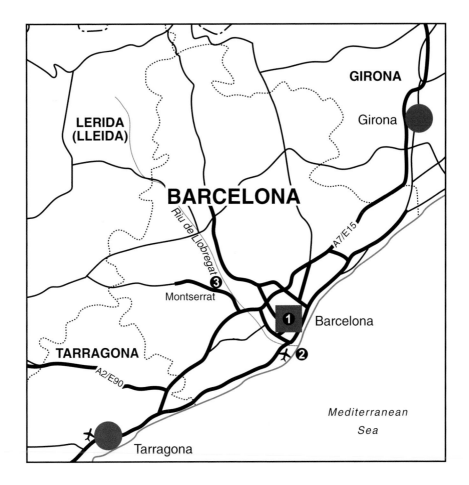

Barcelona

The Province is, of course, totally dominated by Spain's second city, which spreads its tentacles out and up the valleys radiating up towards the Pyrenees. As with Girona, the hinterland consists largely of wooded hills, but the coast of Barcelona Province is almost entirely 'developed,' leaving little room for nature. passage migrants are, of course, likely just about anywhere, and we have included two sites which may be of interest to visitors who, for instance, have to visit the city of Barcelona on a brief business or social trip, and have a few hours to spare.

The traffic you will find in the city is no worse than in most major metropoli, and better than some, but the A7 motorway can be quite hectic, and the entrances and exits to and from the city can be very congested during the rush hour.

The new and rather splendid International Airport at Llobregat serves the city, which also has major rail-connections.

Apart from the sites singled out, the Karst limestone hills behind the coast between Castelldefels and Sitges can repay exploration (Head for the peak shown on the maps as 'Morella.') at any time of year, with a good population of warblers typical of the area, and always the chance of an Eagle Owl or a Bonelli's Eagle.

41

Barcelona Sites

B1. Barcelona City and Surroundings.
B2. Delta de Llobregat.
B3. Montserrat.

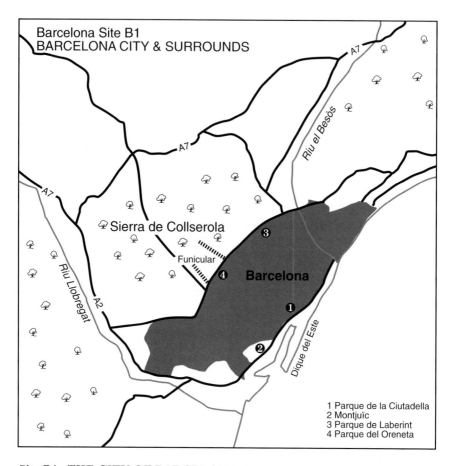

Barcelona Site B1
BARCELONA CITY & SURROUNDS

Sierra de Collserola

Funicular

❹ **Barcelona**

❸

❶

❷

Riu el Besòs

Riu Llobregat

Dique del Este

1 Parque de la Ciutadella
2 Montjuïc
3 Parque de Laberint
4 Parque del Oreneta

Site B1. THE CITY OF BARCELONA

This section is really intended for those who find themselves visiting the city, perhaps on business, and would like to spend a few leisure hours gainfully.

A glance at the map will suffice to show that Barcelona is, in fact, strategically situated on the coast of Cataluña, and it is a city better eqipped with parks and gardens than most.

The port has a long breakwater, the Dique del Este, accessible from the Maritime Station. A protracted seawatch from here in April, for example, can be rewarding, with a good chance of shearwaters, Gannet and some of the scarcer gulls, like Little Gull. This can be combined with a visit to the Parque de la Ciutadella, where Barcelona's zoo is situated, but which boasts, at the time of writing, both species of feral parakeets mentioned in this guide.

Any of the city's parks can boast migrants at passage times, and the gardens below the Olympic Stadium at Montjuic are strategically-placed to receive them.

The higher part of the city abutts the Sierra de Collserola, and two parks are situated along this boundary, the Parque del Laberint (behind the Velodrome), to the north, and the Oreneta, to the south. They both have good birdlife, especially in spring, when Wryneck, Golden Oriole and Melodious Warbler can all be seen here, along with any amount of migrants. Raptors may well be seen passing over, especially on westerly winds.

The whole of the Sierra de Collserola forms a sizeable natural park. Two funicular railways ascend the heights, and the forests are full of Wild Boar and Red Squirrel.

Practical Points

There is no shortage of hotels in Barcelona. Beware frenetic city traffic, and take some care over your personal security – neither better nor worse than other cities of comparable size. At weekends and fiestas, tranquillity in all such parks, right on Barcelona's doorstep, may well be hard to find.

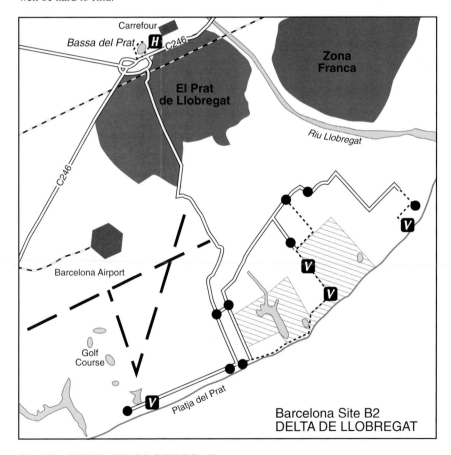

Barcelona Site B2
DELTA DE LLOBREGAT

Site B2. DELTA DE LLOBREGAT

Those who are familiar with some of the less obviously attractive birding sites in Britain may well feel at home here, as this is a site (two sites, really, separated by the new city airport) squashed in between industrial areas, and given to occasional interesting aromas! In common with such equally insalubrious spots as occur in Britain (no names!) it is prone

43

to turn up some excellent birds, especially at passage times. The build-up of winter flocks of Mediterranean Gull is also important. At all times the water-level is a factor upon which the bird-life depends, and the flooded fields can abound with birds when conditions are right.

The best way to approach the Delta is to take the C246 from El Prat de Llobregat towards Castelldefels, and turn off at a sign for 'Camping Toro Bravo' – near where you can park and walk to the beach. The more easterly parts can be approached from El Prat de Llobregat, through industrial estates, following signs for the 'Campo de Golf' and 'Platja'- this route can be complicated, and you should allow time for casting around for the best approach. A small pond, with a hide, right next to the hypermarket 'Carrefour' to the north of the town, is known as the 'Bassa del Prat' and has breeding Little Bittern, amongst other things.

Practical Points
At weekends, half the noisy inhabitants of Barcelona may well seem to be heading your way. It should go without saying that your car may well be a target for opportunist crime, so close to urban areas – leave nothing in it! There is an ample supply of hotels, motels, restaurants and camp-sites in the immediate vicinity.

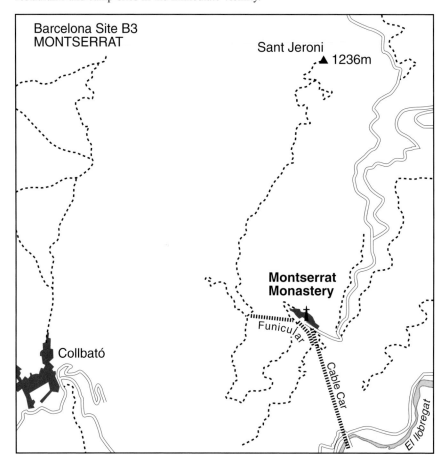

Site B3. MONTSERRAT

Only around 20 kilometres from the centre of the Catalán capital, Montserrat ('sawn-off mountain') is a unique natural environment, one of wierd-shaped rocks, growing abruptly out of largely unspoiled forest and scrub. the monastery of Montserrat itself forms a viewpoint, from where Alpine Swift and Peregrine are not uncommonly seen, and walks amongst the rock-formations can realise a variety of species. Montserrat is known as a wintering area for Wallcreeper and Alpine Accentor. these two prizes are most likely in the area of the summit of Sant Jeroni, a walk of some three kilometres from the top of the funicular railway running from the monastery.

The whole area is worth exploring, and is a veritable treasure, so close to a major city.

Practical Points

A good supply of hotels and restaurants exists nearby. Note that many of the walks shown, particularly in the pamphlets available freely in the area, involve a certain amount of physical effort, as the whole district is hilly in the extreme.

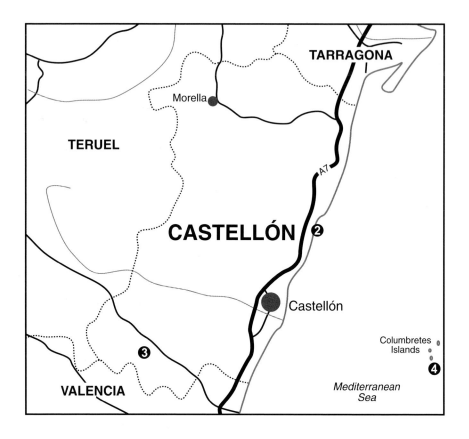

Castellón

This, the northernmost of the three Provinces which go to make up the Valencian Community, is a quite extensive one, with a mountainous interior and a flat coastal plain. Much fruit is grown on the lower slopes of the mountains, whilst the higher areas are often rugged and beautiful. there is the usual ribbon development along the coast road, but the population inland is not very dense. Some lovely old towns are to be found, including the walled fortress of Morella, which is worth a visit in any terms (see C1).

The A7 motorway provides fast and easy access to the whole length of the Province, whilst the roads of the interior tend to be typically slow mountain routes.

Castellon Sites
C1: The Maestrazgo.
C2: Prat de Torreblanca.
C3: Jérica.
C4: Columbretes Islands.

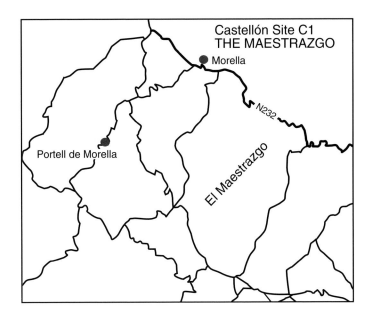

Site C1. THE MAESTRAZGO

This is not so much a 'site' as a whole region, an arm, in fact of the Sistema Ibérico, a range of mountains which stretches from the Ebro southwards, straggling the borders of Teruel and Castellón. The character of the mountains is surprisingly alpine, with stony, tundra-like plateaux, usually snow-covered in winter, and deep, often rocky ravines and river-valleys. This makes for a wild beauty, reinforced by the lack of human population, which is concentrated into a few ancient and very picturesque towns and villages, of which the best is probably Morella. The whole region merits exploration, and it is difficult to single out any one area, but the road westwards from Morella, over high passes to the Portell de Morella and the borders of Teruel is a 'sure thing.' Typically the higher areas sport the local Ortolan Bunting, Tawny Pipit and Rock Thrush, whilst the valleys are good for Dipper, Golden Oriole and warblers. Rock Sparrows are a characteristic bird of the region, and can be seen almost anywhere. Raptors can be hard to find, but there is a good population of Griffon Vultures, and it is possible to find flocks of well over 100 birds. Egyptian Vulture and Booted Eagle are not uncommon, and Short-toed Eagles occur. The higher crags are occupied by Golden and Bonelli's Eagles, and Eagle Owl nest in several places. The extensive forests are home to a very few pairs of Honey Buzzard, and rather more Goshawk and Sparrowhawk. Choughs abound at Morella. The whole region is, incidentally, extremely good for butterflies, and much-frequented by lepidopterists.

Practical Points

Accommodation presents no problem in Morella and other sizeable towns, so long as you avoid the occasional fiestas. Petrol stations, away from these towns, are very few, and it would be an acute embarrassment to run out of fuel on one of the many unsurfaced and remote roads. As with other mountainous zones, sudden changes in weather are liable to occur, and flash-floods are not unknown. Do not get caught in initially dry watercourses when heavy rain threatens! Maps of the area are variable in quality, and apparently good roads can turn abruptly into cart-tracks.

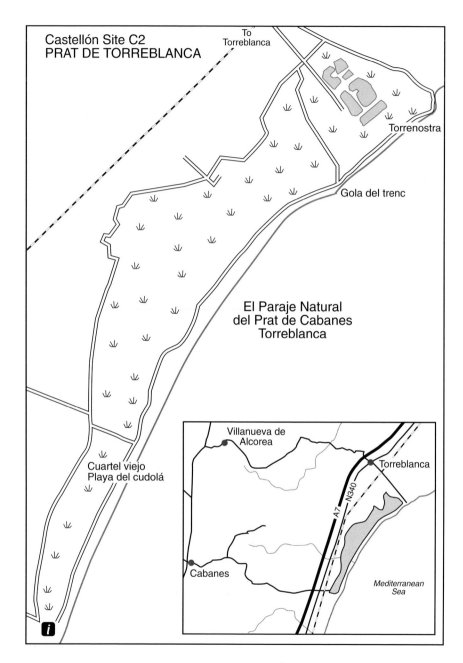

Castellón Site C2
PRAT DE TORREBLANCA

To Torreblanca

Torrenostra

Gola del trenc

El Paraje Natural
del Prat de Cabanes
Torreblanca

Cuartel viejo
Playa del cudolá

Villanueva de
Alcorea

Torreblanca

A7 N340

Cabanes

Mediterranean
Sea

Site C2. PRAT DE TORREBLANCA

This wetland site, also known as El Prat de Cabanes, is especially important as an 'oasis' of wetland and uncultivated, marshy fields, right on the coast north of the provincial capital, Castellón de la Plana. It is reached from the main north-south coast-road, the N340, from the town of Torreblanca, from where you take the road for Torrenostra beach. After passing under a railway bridge, you come axcross the northern boundary of the site, and a laid-out nature trail.

Further south along the N340 is an information centre (seldom open!), reached from Ribera de Cabanes. Walks are possible from this area, and, indeed, around the whole area, including along the beach. Pratincole and Montagu's harrier are amongst the breeding birds, and migration-time is always interesting, but all depends on the highly-variable amount of water to be found in the fields, not forgetting that artificially supplied to the adjoining rice-paddies.

Practical Points

There is ample accommodation along the N340. After rain, some of the tracks can be quite soggy, and quickly become impassable. In summer, the beach and its access points are always crowded, though this usually coincides with drought-conditions and the consequent lack of birds.

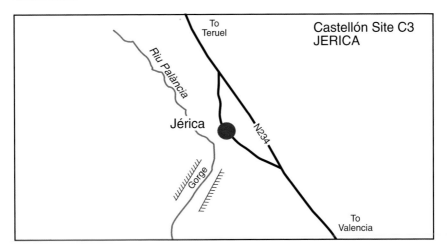

Site C3. JÉRICA

This is not a site which has any particular significance, other than that it is fairly typical of the river-valleys of this region, and is picturesquely-located, near to the through-route from Valencia to Teruel, so that it makes a convenient stopping-place. Simply exploring along the river-bank, into the gorge, will suffice for you to find, in spring, Penduline Tit, Nightingale and Great Reed, Melodious and Cetti's Warbler breeding along the well-vegetated watercourse, and Kingfishers are frequent. Nocturnal raptors are well-represented, and Scop's, Tawny, Long-eared and Eagle Owls are all found here. Nearby hillsides have Nightjar. The scarce Orphean and Olivaceous Warblers both breed (in their respective habitats) and are worth seeking out.

Practical Points

Jérica, a lovely old town, just sufficiently removed from the bustling traffic of the N234, has at least two hostals, and others may be found along the highway, a busy north-south route.

Site C4. COLUMBRETES ISLANDS

The inclusion of these islands in this guide may be of little more than academic importance to a majority of readers, but, should you get the opportunity to pay a visit, especially at migration times, this should not be missed.

The islands, situated at some 28 miles due east of the Cabo de Oropesa, consist of some dozen or so uninhabited and largely inhospitable rocks, the largest of which, the Columbrete Grande, is about a mile in length, and horseshoe-shaped. Landing on the islands is strictly controlled, in order to protect the sensitive indigenous fauna, and is, in any case, extremely hazardous. There are ruins and a lighthouse on the main island, and some study, including annual ringing, is carried out.

The breeding species are few – Yellow-legged and Audouin's Gulls, Cory's Shearwater, Storm Petrel, House Sparrow, and Eleonora's Falcon being annual breeders, whilst Shag may have bred, and may do so in the future.

However, migrants are found in abundance at the right time, and records of such as Lapland Bunting, Wallcreeper and Desert Wheatear are just three examples of the sort of species which can occur at such isolated islands.

Practical Points

Boats can be chartered at Oropesa for non-landing visits, which would certainly give you a chance of seeing the resident Eleonora's Falcons. For a longer-term, study visit, officials of the Medio Ambiente should be contacted, and information can be obtained by writing to:–

Estación Ornitología Albufera, Av. Los Pinares 106, 46012 Valencia.

Audoin's Gull

Cuenca

Although much of this landlocked Province lies outside the scope of this guide, it is worthy of mention, as most of it can be reached on a day-trip from the coast, and a couple of sites have considerable importance. One of the sites, more properly, belongs to Valencia, as the odd little, isolated pocket known as the Rincón de Ademuz, is administratively, a part of that Province, but the site sits, in fact, right across the border between the two. Much of Cuenca's land area is dedicated to cereal-farming, and is therefore home to larks, sparrows and little else, but the Serranía de Cuenca is a low range of hills, with strange sandstone outcrops, formed into sometimes wierd shapes. These form a considerable tourist-attraction to visitors to the region, as does the wonderful Medieval city of Cuenca, with its famous 'hanging houses.' The Valencia-Madrid highway runs through the southern section of the Province, from where the northern parts are accessible on reasonable – if sometimes narrow and poorly-surfaced – roads.

Cuenca Sites
CU1: Moya.
CU2: Hoces de Cabriel.

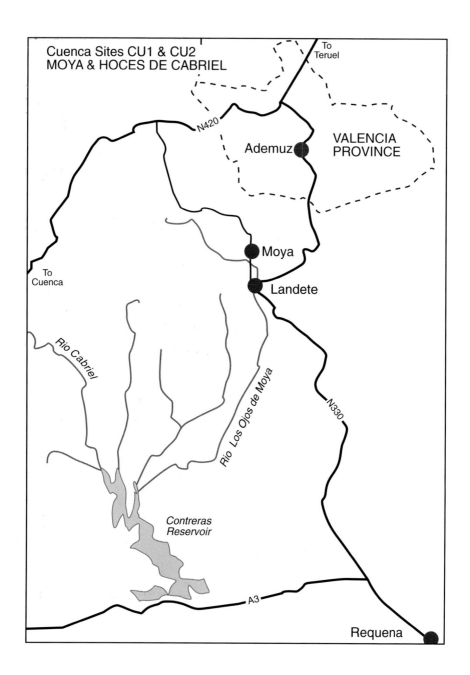

Site CU1. MOYA

This unfrequented corner of Cuenca Province probably has more sites worthy of note, but we pick this one out, because it is useful for its variety, as well as for the presence of Dupont's Lark.

Moya itself is a ruined citadel, something of a minor tourist attraction, on top of a prominent hill, to the north of the agricultural town of Landete. Around the ruins are lots of Rock Sparrows, Black-eared Wheatear and Thekla Lark, whilst the uncultivated areas around the cereal fields at lower levels are the spots to find the elusive Dupont's Lark. Short-toed and Calandra Larks also occur here, and Buzzards are common in the nearby valley.

Travelling out of Landete to the northeast, towards Ademuz, you emerge onto a high plateau, where you cross the border into the Rincon de Ademuz (Valencia Province). Near this point, there is another site for Dupont's Lark, which can be heard calling from the esparto-grass.

Practical Points

There are bars and at least one restaurant in Landete, but the nearest accommodation is to be found in Ademuz. The whole region is very underpopulated, and it pays to make sure you are well supplied with fuel and drink before you undertake adventures off the beaten track.

Site CU2. HOCES DE CABRIEL

The lonely river valleys around the northern end of the large (and unexciting) reservoir of Contreras, are worth looking at – though no better, it has to be said, than others further to the northwest of the Province – and have populations of raptors, including Egyptian Vulture, Peregrine, Bonelli's and Booted Eagles, as well as Eagle Owls and Alpine Swift. There are obvious cliffs in these river-valleys, and the valleys themselves have Great Spotted Woodpecker, Melodious Warbler and Golden Oriole.

Practical Points

Cuenca has ample accommodation, just so long as you avoid the city's famous fiestas, and is a beautiful and fascinating – if touristy – city. Elsewhere, the region is very sparsely populated, with few facilities of any kind. It can be seriously hot in summer.

Thekla Lark

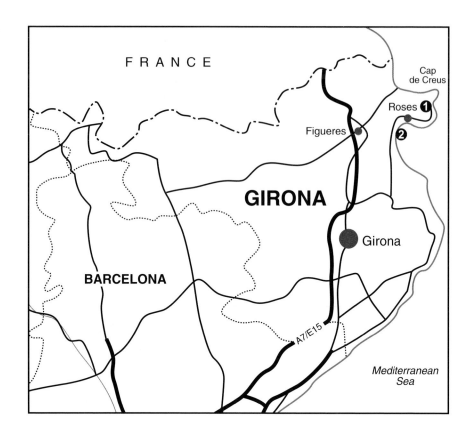

Girona

Slightly confusingly, this Province, at the northeastern extremity of Spain was, until recently, known as Gerona, and its car-numbers carried the prefix 'GE.' With the passing of the Franco era, this has all changed, and Catalan is now the official language (see the chapter on Customs and Culture) – so now we have to call it by its Catalan equivalent.

As stated in our introduction, we are confining ourselves to the coastal strip for these Catalan Provinces. For that reason, we shall only treat two sites as worthy of special treatment, although there are plenty of spots where a sea-watch would not go amiss, and the area at the back of Estartit has turned up some good birds in the past.

The Province of Girona is of average size, with a well-wooded, mountainous hinterland, and a rugged coastline, interspersed with some hideously overdeveloped seaside resorts, where the undeniably fine beaches have attracted hordes of tourists, in ever-increasing numbers, since the inception of the 'package-tour.' There remain some very attractive little resorts, such as the port of Cadaqués, famed as the home of Salvador Dali, but such places have become quite chic and therefore expensive. The resorts of Tossa and Lloret will require little introduction to the reader of holiday brochures, and will probably have scant attraction for the reader of this guide!

Inland, the areas of wooded hills tend to be largely unrewarding from a birding viewpoint – that is, until one reaches the higher foothills of the Pyrenees, towards the borders of Lleida (Lérida) Province. The Pyrenees are well-covered in 'A Birdwatching Guide to the

Pyrenees' (Arlequin Press) and it will suffice to mention that the Valle de Freser, north of Ripoll, is probably the furthest east for Lammergeier, as well as having other raptors.

If you are driving down from France, you will enter Girona on the extremely busy north-south motorway, though the coastal N114 is a slower alternative, with accommodation to be found at the unattractive coastal town of Colera. If, on the other hand, you are approaching from Andorra, you should allow lots of time for the mountain roads which wind down through the ski-resorts of Molina.

The air-traveller will probably arrive at Girona airport, which is served by charter-flights from the UK and elsewhere.

Girona Sites
G1. Cabo de Creus.
G2. Aiguamolls de l'Empdora.

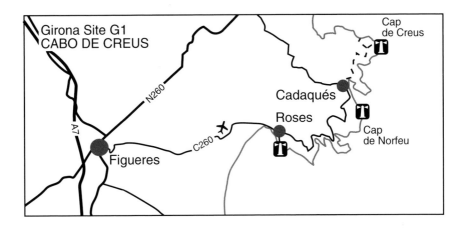

Site G1. CABO DE CREUS
This, the easternmost point of the Iberian peninsula, is a rocky headland, with many semi-submerged rocks and little islets, just offshore. the headland, and other, associated ones nearby, are covered with Mediterranean scrub in parts, whilst other areas are basically stony, overgrazed, plains.

Like many headlands, some footwork is advisable, and the access to paths is obvious, approaching the easterly, main, headland from Cadaqués, and the associated Cabo Norfeo from Roses (Rosas). Much depends, of course, upon weather conditions, as to which site is the better, and the whole area is worth close inspection.

Resident species are predictably few, but contain birds of much interest to the northern visitor. Warblers are mainly restricted to the *Sylvia* species, with Spectacled in the lower scrub, Subalpine inhabiting the larger bushes, and the elusive Orphean in the pines. Thekla Lark, Ortolan Bunting, and Red-rumped Swallow breed in the area, but the population of Lesser Kestrels is sadly a thing of the past. The sea-cliffs have populations of Pallid Swift, Blue Rock Thrush and Black Wheatear, and a sea-watch may well be rewarded, at virtually any season, with views of Shag, and shearwaters. Passage is, of course, exciting in this prominent site, and seabirds can include the odd Kittiwake or sea-duck. The list of passerine migrants seen here is huge.

Winter brings with it the chance of a Wallcreeper, probably in one of the several stone-quarries found here.

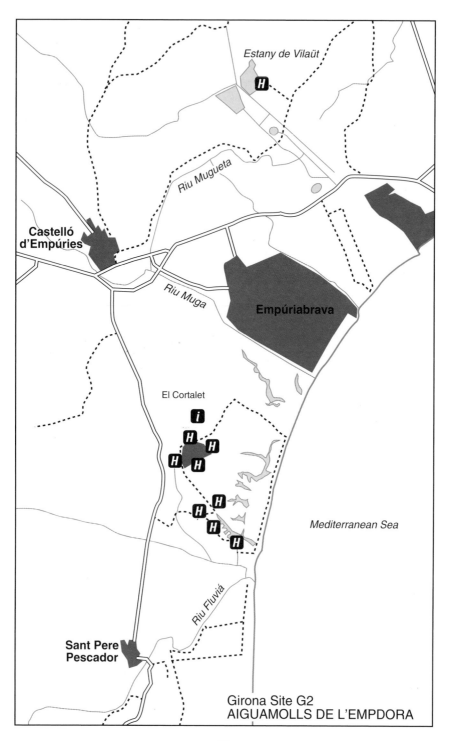

Estany de Vilaüt

Riu Mugueta

Castelló
d'Empúries

Riu Muga

Empúriabrava

El Cortalet

Mediterranean Sea

Riu Fluvià

Sant Pere
Pescador

Girona Site G2
AIGUAMOLLS DE L'EMPDORA

56

Practical Points

Accommodation is no problem in the fashionable and picturesque coastal town of Cadaqués, with its Dali connections, and there are plenty of hotels in Rosas, but reservations are usually necessary in summer, or the week prior to Easter. (Semana Santa)

The proximity of this site to Aiguamolls (G2) makes a combined holiday more than feasible. Allow plenty of time!

Site G2. AIGUAMOLLS DE L'EMPORDÁ

This hugely-important site is second only to the Ebro Delta as a place to see a whole range of species in Cataluña, and, situated so close to the French frontier, is bound to attract many visiting birders. It is simple of access, being a question of leaving the A-7 motorway, or the N-2 highway, and taking the exit signposted for Figueres, which you circumnavigate, then continue on the C-260 towards Roses. Roughly halfway from Castelló d'Empuries to Sant Pere Pescador, and after passing a petrol station, you take a left turn, signed to the Information Centre, which is open from 9.30 to 2, and from 3.30 to 6 between October and March, but only from 4.30 to 7 during the warmer months. Maps and guides in many languages are available here, at 'El Cortalet.'

The lagoons of Aiguamolls are, in fact, vestiges of a once more extensive coastal marsh, at the mouths of the two rivers, the Fluviá and the Muga. A strenuous local campaign resulted in the declaration of reserve status in 1983.

The southernmost area is accessible from the Information Centre, from where a nature trail goes right around the area, giving access to some eight hides. The whole round trip could well be a long morning's work. (more at passage-time!) 'Camargue' horses graze much of the area, but ornithological interest is considerable. The park's emblem, the Garganey, breeds here and nowhere else in Spain, whilst there is a healthy population of Purple Gallinule. White Stork feed commonly as their local population increases, and there is almost always a Marsh Harrier to be seen. The rarer crakes are also possible. In winter, when access to the beach is unrestricted (it is closed during the breeding season, to allow nesting birds some peace) this can be a good spot to see divers and sea-ducks, as well as wintering waders, possibly including Glossy Ibis. raptors are also common in winter.

The more northerly area necessitates a trip back to Castelló d'Empuries.After crossing the river, following signs to Roses, take a left turn along the Riu Mugueta. After crossing the marsh, there is a track to a hide overlooking the Estany de Vilaüt, a little freshwater pool, of which there are several in the area. Here Bittern, Little Bittern, Purple Heron and Purple Gallinule may be found, and it may well be the best place for the local Lesser Grey Shrike.

Tracks and lesser roads cross the whole area from Empúries in the south to the outskirts of Roses in the north, and many merit exploration. Allow plenty of time for this fine area.

Practical Points

There are plenty of hostals and hotels in the area – it may be easier to find accommodation in the less fashionable towns of Castelló d'Empuries or Sant Pere Pescador, than in the popular coastal resorts.

Tarragona

Tarragona is a narrower Province than its two Catalan neighbours to the north, not extending northwards right up to the Pyrenees. The coastal strip is quite heavily built up to the northeast, thinning out a bit as one leaves the Provincial capital to the southwest, and culminating in the massively-important Ebro Delta, whose rice-fields feed much of the Spanish appetite for that vegetable. Inland, it is a sunny Province, with much area given over to wine-growing, but with some surprisingly rocky mountains, which are worth exploring if you have the time.

Communications are particularly good here, with the coastal motorway, the A7, affording fast access from Barcelona to the north, and from Valencia to the south. The Madrid-bound A2 joins it at the northeastern extremity of the Province. Air-travellers are served by the airport at Reus, which carries package-deal flights from the UK and elsewhere.

Tarragona Sites
T1. The Ebro Delta.
T2. Puertos de Tortosa.

58

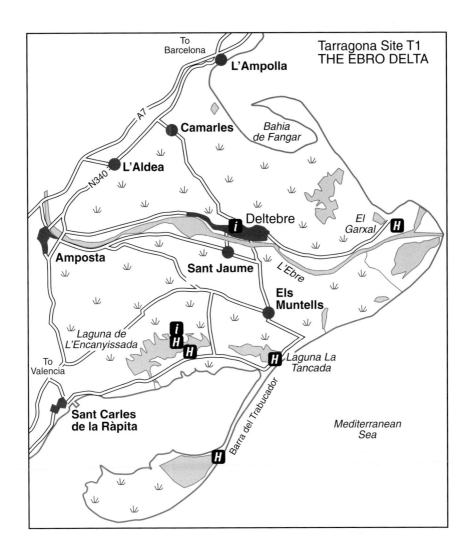

Site T1. THE EBRO DELTA

This is, of course, a site of major, international, importance, being one of the great Mediterranean wetlands, even after many years of exploitation. Of its 32,000 hectares, in fact some 20,000 are under cultivation, but the universal crop is rice, and flooded rice paddies can be of importance for resting and feeding waders and herons. There are, however, areas set aside for conservation, which is here taken quite seriously, with major lagoons and reedbeds occupying a major part of the delta area. There are also plans afoot to improve the regimes of rice cultivation along ecological lines, wherever such measures can be introduced. It is, however, a constant battle (conservation v. money!) and it is not even close to being won.

We can conveniently separate the northern and southern parts of the delta, with the river itself as a boundary. (This is crossed by a series of rather primitive car-ferries, which carry on a continuous service during daylight hours, and are found along the river in the neighbourhood of San Jaime, where they are well-signposted).

The Northern Areas

There is an Information Centre at Deltebre (which you may be lucky enough to find open, and where you can obtain detailed maps and publicity, though it is unlikely you will find anyone who knows 'what is about.' You can head out to the northeast from here, and cross the vast area of ricefields, where herons, waders and other species should be found, to the coast, and footpath which traces the sandbar at the northern edge of the 'Bahia de Fangal'. this path will take a couple of hours to walk, and can be cold and windy in winter – the best time, however. Then birds unusual in Spain, such as Eider and scoters , are to be looked for, and Red-breasted Merganser are frequent. At passage times, waders, skuas and terns are good here. A few pair of Oystercatcher breed, as do Kentish Plover. The tern colonies should be treated with suitable respect.

Back at the Information Centre, try travelling due east along the main arm of the river, to the tourist-trap area near the mouth itself. here you can ditch any of your party who may wish to buy tacky souvenirs, or take a riverboat trip, and take a walk alongside the big saline lagoon of Garxal. Gulls and terns here can be excellent, being an area for Slender-billed and Audouin's Gull, whilst Caspian Tern are regular. Migrants are often to be found here, and Pratincole, Osprey and many passerines should be yielded up by a visit at migration times. There is usually a good flock of Red-crested Pochard here, and grebes are also numerous.

The Southern Part

At least a day is required to do any justice at all to this part of the Delta alone, and you can explore the whole region for several days without becoming bored. There is a 'Mirador' – observation-tower – at the Laguna de l'Encanyissada, from which the variety of wildfowl, herons and other species can be sensational. Marsh Harriers quarter the reeds at virtually any season, and terns, herons and waders abound. The ricefields of La Noria are very good, especially in spring and autumn, when herons and terns are a feature.

Striking outeastwards to the coast from here, you come across the huge Laguna de la Tancada, where there is another observation point, but you will do much watching from your vehicle, and the big gatherings of resting gulls and terns are always worth a scan. This is the best area for waders, too.

You can then take the ride southwards along the Barra del Trabucador, towards the salinas, to which entry is prohibited. This involves a long trip along unmade roads, which are, however, normally sound enough. From this track, and the observatory at the end, you can usually find such species as Audouin's and Slender-billed Gull, whilst caspian and even Lesser Crested Tern are frequent at appropriate times. Big gatherings of Flamingo are normal here too.

Practical Points

There are ample opportunities in terms of accommodation at Amposta and Sant Carles de la Ràpita, and campsites are to be found at several points, as well as signs advertising rooms to let. Caution should be observed when stopping on the narrow roads throughout the delta, as traffic can be surprisingly heavy, especially at weekends. Flies and mosquitoes are present in squadrons, and you may wish to choose your picnic sites accordingly.

No 'wild' camping is permitted within the Delta area, but there are organised campsites, well signposted.

Should you wish to consult with the authorities who control the National Park, their telephone number is 977-48-96-79, and they can arrange guided visits, should you so require – though it must be borne in mind that Spanish guided tours can be noisy, social affairs! The number of the Tourist Information Office, at Sant Carles de Rápita is 977-74-01-00. The other ayuntamientos (adjuntaments in Catalán) or town halls in the area all have their own tourism services.

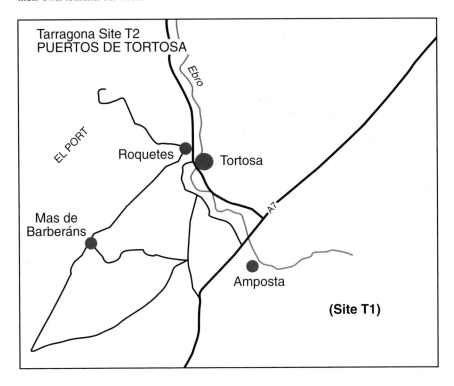

Site T2. PORTS DE TORTOSA

This site is really almost a continuation into Cataluña of the Maestrazgo (see Castellón), being, geologically, a part of the Sistema Ibérico. It is included here because a visit to the area can easily be combined with a holiday in the nearby Ebro Delta (T1).

A road ascends the wilder 'barrancos' from just south of Mas de Barberans, and another leaves the minor road west from Roquetes, at four kilometres from that village. these can both be explored at will. A scattering of all the raptors you would expect inhabits this area, and Eagle Owl are well-represented in the 'barrancos.' Both Nightjars breed on the scrub-covered hillsides, and the warbler families are particularly good here, with the scarce Orphean not uncommon. Wintering Wallcreeper, Citril Finch and Alpine Accentor are to be looked for in the higher parts, where the breeding season is good for Tawny Pipit and Ortolan Bunting.

Practical Points

Tortosa is a small but busy town, with several hotels and plenty of bars and restaurants.

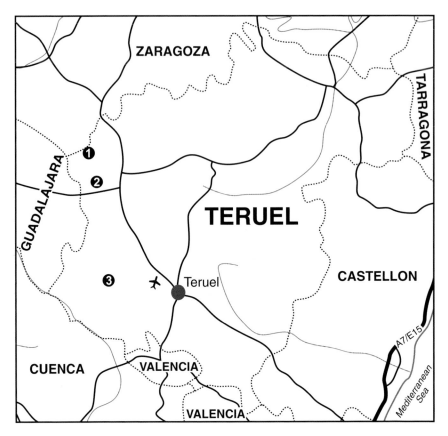

Teruel

The Province of Teruel is the southernmost of the three Provinces of Aragón. (the others are Zaragoza and Huesca) It is a big, underpopulated Province, with seemingly limitless plains and wild mountains, rising to quite impressive heights – the ski-resort of Valdelinares has peaks of close to 2,000 metres in its area. Much of the Province is covered by a sparse growth of rather sombre-looking 'encinas' (evergreen oaks), but the stony plains provide a stark contrast. Some of the river valleys are planted with poplars, and the little streams give rise to some good patches of vegetation. Cereals are grown on a large scale here, especially in the north of the Province, and ham and ham-products are widely regarded as some of the best in Spain.

The region was the scene of much bitter fighting in the Civil War, and the harsh winter climate did nothing to make this a pleasurable experience, as fans of Laurie Lee will know. Teruel itself is an imposing capital city, but the other towns are small and largely agricultural. Rubielos de Mora is an absolute gem, and is easily confused with the nearby Mora de Rubielos (!) which is ordinary in the extreme.

The busy but reasonably quick N234 bisects the Province, and is a major lorry-route from the fruit-growing south to Northern Europe.

Apart from the sites given here, many of the river valleys are well worth a little time, but many apparently suitable mountain regions seem largely devoid of birds. As with all such areas, a modicum of patience, and a deal of luck will be necessary.

Teruel Sites

TE1. Gallocanta Area (On the border of Zaragoza Province).

TE2. Blancas/Odon/Torralba Area.

TE3. The Albarracín Area.

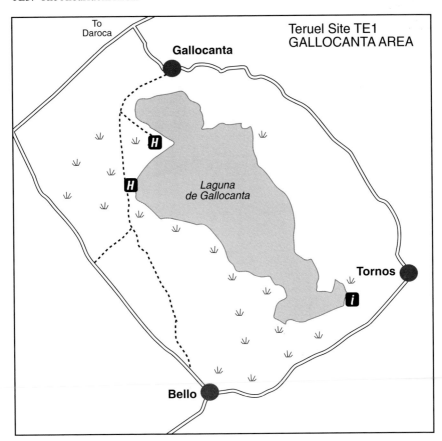

Site TE1. GALLOCABTA AND AREA

Gallocanta is the largest NATURAL lake in Spain – there are plenty of bigger reservoirs, of course – but has the problem it shares with many endorreic lagoons, namely, lack of water! Most years it dries out totally, and looks more suited to a world land-speed record attempt than to birding! If, however, the autumn rains arrive in time, the Crane population, as they make their way south, can reach many thousands, and the water can hold large wintering numbers of duck,as well as a lot of waders, both in winter and on passage.

Even if, however, the water is non-existent, the surrounding areas are always worth a visit. leaving the primitive village of Gallocanta on an indifferent track, you head for a rocky promontory at the northwestern end of the lake (best viewing, of course, in the evening). Here Rock Sparrow flocks are common, Tree Sparrows too can sometimes be found, and the rocks seem to attract migrants. There is a reserve 'observation point' here, and, looking out across the fields and the lake, harriers are usually to be seen, together with other raptors, depending upon season. Dropping down to the southwestern shore, there are usually (outside the breeding season) flocks of larks – Calandra and Skylark prominent amongst them – Corn Buntings, and always the chance of Black-bellied Sandgrouse and both bustards. If there are to be Cranes about, this area is perhaps the best one.

At the southeastern end of the lake, there is an Information Centre, (which always seems to be closed!), and you can approach the water, when there is some, quite closely at various points on the lake's perimeter. Tracks are a good alternative to the road, virtually all the way around, but the point about the northwestern end is that you can gain elevation, thereby commanding a decent view.

Practical Points

There are few facilities in the area, although the villages do have a bar apiece, at least. The best bet for accommodation is Daroca, some half-hour's drive to the northeast from Gallocanta. It is a site to visit, normally, outside the breeding season, of course, but, should you venture there in midsummer, expect high temperatures and heat-haze.

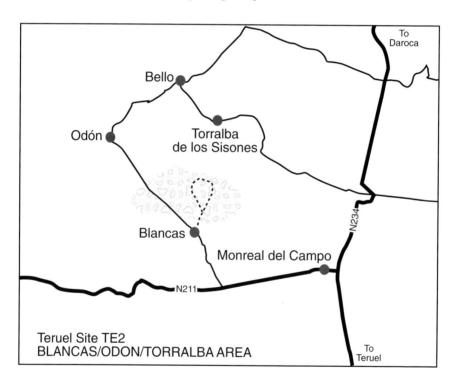

Teruel Site TE2
BLANCAS/ODON/TORRALBA AREA

Site TE2. BLANCAS, VILLALBA, ODON AREAS

This is really best regarded as a site best visited as part of a trip to Gallocanta (q.v.), just to the north of this area.

Although not shown on the Michelin map, a road joins Blanca to Torralba de los Sisones (White Tower of the Little Bustards!), making a square, with Bello, near the edge of Gallocanta, and Odón as the other corners. A gentle ride around the square, especially in spring, should help you find a nice selection of birds, including Hen Harrier, shrikes, Rock Sparrow, Ortolan Bunting and wheatears. To the north of the village of Blancas, you can find your way out onto a stony wasteland (leave the village, going due north, on an unlikely-looking track, which heads past an unattractive rubbish-dump), with a good density of breeding Dupont's, Lesser Short-toed and Short-toed Larks, Stone Curlew, and Black-bellied Sandgrouse. Raven, Chough and sometimes Golden Eagle are to be seen over this excellent area.

Practical Points
Unmade roads in this part of the world are apt to be sharp, stony, affairs – make sure your spare tyre is OK! It is a lonely area, without gas-stations or restaurants, but the busy N234 is not far away. The Hostal Botero, at Monreal del Campo, provides excellent accommodation at reasonable prices.

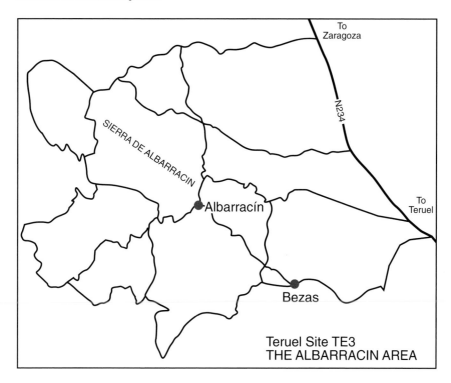

Teruel Site TE3
THE ALBARRACIN AREA

Site TE3. THE ABERRACÍN AREA
Alberracín is a major tourist attraction, a town with Moorish walls constructed between the tenth and fourteenth centuries. The town itself dates back to only a few centuries later, and is a medieval delight. The valleys around the town are of great ornithological interest, and Egyptian Vulture, Bonelli's Eagle and Peregrine nest in the cliffs, together with big numbers of Rock Sparrow, whilst Cirl, Rock and Ortolan Buntings are found higher up. The valley bottoms are good for warblers, Great Spotted Woodpecker and Golden Oriole, and the pinewoods hold Crested Tit and a small breeding population of Siskin. Autumn sees an influx of Buzzards from further north. Cave-paintings some 8,000 years old, to be seen just off the road to Bezas (at 4 kilometres from the town) are an added attraction.

Practical Points

Accommodation is plentiful in and around Alberracín. The Hotel Montes Universales, just outside the town on the Teruel road is reasonably-priced and comfortable. Although an apparent 'tourist-trap' prices are generally not too high. The area can experience very high midday temperatures, and early-morning birding is the best.

Short-toed Eagle

Valencia

Valencia is the third largest city in the land, and, like Barcelona, spreads out, though not in the way, perhaps, that a British city would, and it can be surprisingly rural just a few kilometres from the city. We only treat three wetlands as separate sites here, and they are of some importance, but that is not to infer that the rest of the Province is birdless. the interior of Valencia, in fact, is rugged and beautiful in parts, and many typical mountain species are to be found, particularly in the montane areas to the southeast of Cofrentes. The coastal plains are much given to rice production, especially around the Albufera, and the Province is world-famous for its oranges, whose groves cloak the hillsides for much of the region. Higher up, almonds take over.

Valencia airport is a major international one, with regular flights from the UK, but less charter operations than Alicante. The A7 motorway runs right along the coast, and is free of tolls where it passes by the city.

Valencia Sites
V1: Marjal del Moro.
V2: Albufera de Valencia.
V3: Pego (part in Alicante).

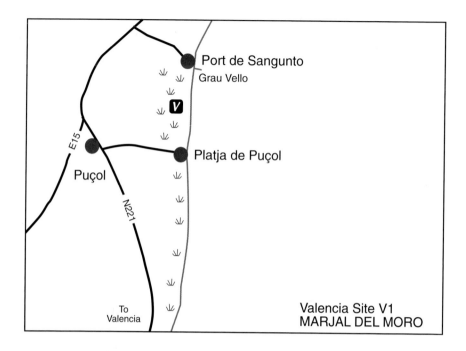

Port de Sangunto
Grau Vello

Platja de Puçol

Puçol

E15

N221

To
Valencia

Valencia Site V1
MARJAL DEL MORO

Site V1. MARJAL DEL MORO

This is a coastal wetland, of some importance, no more than 30 kilometres from the centre of Valencia, and a similar distance from the airport.

Two approaches are possible. From the south, when you take the road to the Playa de Puçol, from the centre of Puçol. When you hit the coast, turn left, and proceed to beyond the end of the tarmac road, when you will be virtually on the reserve, and you will see a raised observation platform at the edge of a small pond. You can reach this point from the north, too, by dint of taking the road signposted for the Puerto de Sagunto, just south of that town. When you get to the roundabout just before a huge factory, turn right towards Valencia, then take a left, on unmade roads, for the 'Grau vella' (old jetty), where you reach the coast. the beach is shingle here, and it is common to see coasting gulls, shearwaters and so forth from this point.

The reserve features an extensive system of reedbeds and open water, and is reliable for Purple Gallinule (especially in the mornings, when you should see them from the observation tower.)

Collared Pratincole breed, as do small numbers of Whiskered Terns, and most of the herons, including Squacco and Little Bittern. Situated as it is, there is always the chance of a good wader here, and passage of passerines can be interesting. Savi's Warbler is a breeding species, and almost anything can turn up here.

Practical Points

The road along the coast is rough, though perfectly passable. Accommodation is available in the form of hostals and hotels in Sagunto and Puçol, though the latter is a busy little town, with some pestilential traffic lights. Mosquitoes can be interesting here, especially on spring evenings.

Plate 9. Peñon de Ifach & Salinas de Calpe.

Plate 10. Font Roja, Alicante.

Plate 11. Sierra de Salinas, Alicante.

Plate 12. Sierras de Alicante.

Plate 13. Salinas de Santa Pola.

Plate 14. Salinas de Santa Pola.

Plate 15. El Hondo.

Plate 16. La Mata.

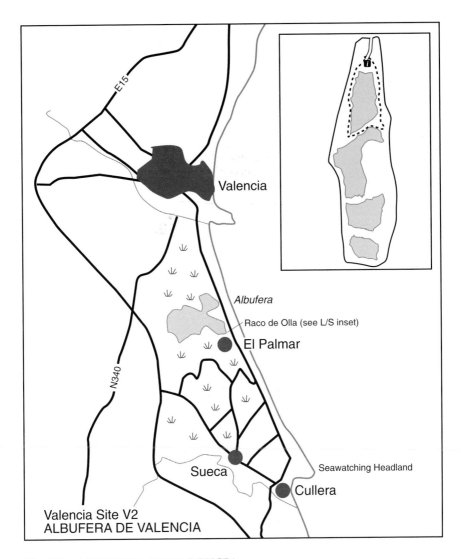

Valencia

Albufera

Raco de Olla (see L/S inset)

El Palmar

N340

E15

Sueca

Seawatching Headland

Cullera

Valencia Site V2
ALBUFERA DE VALENCIA

Site V2. ALBUFERA DE VALENCIA

The Albufera is one of the most important stretches of wetland on the whole coast, but it is not particularly 'user-friendly' when it comes to finding birds

Having said that, the Valencian authorities have set up an excellent little reserve at the 'Raco de Olla' – just off the V15 road, near the Parador, south of El Saler. Here you can scale a small tower for a distant view across the huge expanse of fresh water which comprimises much of the reserve, but this is only really useful for seeing large birds like raptors. There is also a hide and nature trail, centred on a little, marshy pond – good for waders and the odd migrant (the woods here are often teeming with migrants in season).

For more opportunities to see the best birds on offer here, drive on past the Raco de Olla, and through the amazing little town of El Palmar (totally dedicated to feeding you!), turning right at the very end. From here, you can explore the network of tracks – and some surfaced roads – which extend out over the rice fields. When these are flooded, in the spring, they can be great for views of the increasing numbers of Glossy Ibis, for roosing Audoin's Gull, terns including Gull-billed, and a wide variety of herons and waders. You can explore some of these tracks on foot, too, and there are boat excursions to be had from El Palmar. When the fields dry out, however, later in the year, the birds disperse, often, it seems, to inaccessible places.

Practical Points

Accommodation is, of course, no problem in an area so dedicated to tourism, with hotels and campsites all along the coast. Anyone who goes hungry, anywhere near El Palmar, will have only himself to blame! Do please note that the car park at the Raco de Olla is notorious for robberies from vehicles – LEAVE NOTHING for the thieves.

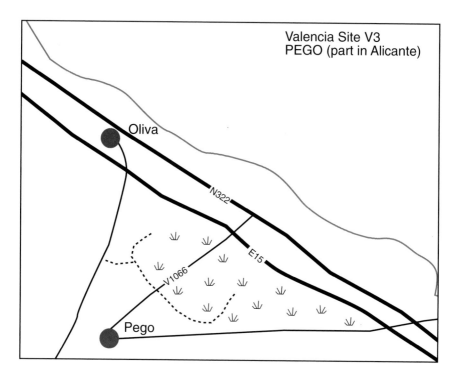

Site V3. PEGO MARSH (PART IN ALICANTE)

This marsh, or the remnants of it, is crossed by the V1066 road, between the N332 coast road and Pego village. There are several tracks which can be taken across it, but they are often barred to vehicular traffic, probably by the cattle-farmers, who use parts of it as grazing marsh. these are the best parts, in general, as much of the rest has been lost to 'agricultural vandalism' in recent years.

However, a small population of Purple Gallinule still hangs on here, and a very few pairs of Marbled Duck breed. In winter, Penduline Tit and Bluethroat are numerous, and herons, waders and raptors are normally about. A small breeding population of feral Waxbills existed until recently, and may still be there, and there is always a chance of a glimpse of one of the rarer crakes, as it crosses the open paths and cuts which cross the marsh.

Kingfishers are common in winter, and Little Ringed Plover, Ruff and Green Sandpiper are often to be seen around the flowing water.

Practical Points

Accommodation is readily available along the N332. Hunters and fisherman make great use of what is left of the marshland. Do not antagonise them – they may be its only hope of survival! You should not try to park on the road which crosses the marsh – there are places where you can tuck your car off the road.

Black-winged Stilts

Rapid Guide to 'Key' Species

This chapter is designed to help those who are unfamiliar with the region – and Spain as a whole – and who may have limited time at their disposal, and therefore wish to plan some kind of a 'lightning raid.'

We therefore concentrate upon the characteristic species of the region, and particularly those unlikely to be found elsewhere.

The list is necessarily subjective, and reflects the authors' experience as to which site may present the best chance of seeing the species, for a minimum expenditure of time.

It should be borne in mind that many sites change dramatically from year to year, especially where they depend upon water-levels. Good luck!

(Column three attempts to assess your chance, on a scale of 1-10, of seeing the bird, on a visit of four hour's duration, at the right time.)

Season: Winter = 1, Spring = 2, Summer = 3, Autumn = 4.

Where more than one site is mentioned, the first-named represents your best chance.

Species	Recommended site(s)	/10	Season
Cory's Shearwater	Cabo de la Nao, or any coastal site	3	2,4
Little Bittern	El Hondo, Marjal del Moro	8	2,3
Night Heron	Ebro Delta, Albufera, El Hondo	4	2,3,4
Squacco Heron	Ebro Delta, El Hondo	6	2,3,4
Purple Heron	Ebro Delta, El Hondo, Santa Pola	10	2,3
Glossy Ibis	Albufera, El Hondo	5	Any
Greater Flamingo	Ebro Delta, Santa Pola	10	Any
Marbled Duck	El Hondo	9	2,3,4*
Ferruginous Duck	Ebro Delta, Albufera	2	Any
White-headed Duck	El Hondo	7	2,3,4*
Egyptian Vulture	Maestrazgo, Ports de Tortosa	8	3
Griffon Vulture	Maestrazgo, Gallocanta	9	Any
Short-toed Eagle	Maestrazgo, Ports de Tortosa	5	2,3
Booted Eagle	Maestrazgo, etc.	8	2,3,4
	El Hondo	10	1
Bonelli's Eagle	Northern Sierras of Alicante	6	Any
Eleonora's Falcon	Columbretes	10	3,4
Purple Gallinule	Aiguamolls, Marjal del Moro	9	Any
Little Bustard	Gallocanta, Pétrola	3	1,2*
Great Bustard	Pétrola, Gallocanta	6	1,3,4*
Collared Pratincole	El Hondo, Ebro Delta	10	3
Slender-billed Gull	Santa Pola Salinas	10	Any
Audouin's Gull	Ebro Delta, Albufera, Santa Pola	9	Any
Gull-billed Tern	Ebro Delta, Pétrola, Albufera	5	2,3
Caspian Tern	Ebro Delta, Albufera, Santa Pola	2	Any
Lesser Crested Tern	Ebro Delta, Albufera, Santa Pola	1	3,4
Whiskered Tern	El Hondo, Marjal del Moro	10	2,3*
Black-bellied Sandgrouse	Gallocanta	6	Any
Pin-tailed Sandgrouse	Pétrola	3	1,4*
Great Spotted Cuckoo	Pétrola, almost anywhere	4	2,3
Scops Owl	Gardens in towns (at night!)	3	2,3
Eagle Owl	Maestrazgo, etc. (at night!)	1	Any
Red-necked Nightjar	Sierra de Santa Pola (at night)	10	3
Pallid Swift	Cabo de la Nao, Tabarca	10	2,3
Alpine Swift	Alcala del Júcar, Maestrazgo	9	2,3,4
Roller	Aiguamolls, other coastal sites	4	2*

Species	Recommended site(s)	/10	Season
Dupont's Lark	Blancas, Moya	3	Any+
Calandra Lark	Gallocanta, Pétrola	8	1,2,4*
Lesser Short-toed Lark	El Hondo, Blancas	9	Any+
Thekla Lark	Sierra de Santa Pola, etc.	10	Any+
Red-rumped Swallow	Just about anywhere!	5	2*
Rufous Bush Robin	Sierra de Santa Pola	7	3+
Black-eared Wheatear	Cabo de la Nao, Sierra de Santa Pola, etc.	10	2,3
Black Wheatear	As above	10	Any
Rock Thrush	Maestrazgo	4	3
Blue Rock Thrush	Cabo de la Nao, Santa Pola, etc.	10	Any
Savi's Warbler	Marjal del Moro	4	3+
Moustached Warbler	El Hondo, Marjal del Moro	6	1,2*+
Olivaceous Warbler	Guardamar, etc.	2	3+
Orphean Warbler	Jérica, Sierra de Salinas	2	3
Penduline Tit	El Hondo	8	1*+
Lesser Grey Shrike	Aiguamolls	7	3
Rock Sparrow	Gallocanta, Blancas	8	Any
Rock Bunting	Maestrazgo etc.	7	Any

NB: * denotes a species which may well be present outside the seasons shown, but that those times will give your best chance of finding the bird.

+ denotes a species where familiarity with the species' vocabulary is normally essential for its location/identification.

Specific List

This list contains all species known to have been recorded in the area covered by this guide, within recent years. For scientific and Spanish names, refer to the 'tick-list.' It should, perhaps, be borne in mind that Spain is not nearly so organised as some Northern European nations, in the matter of recording and there is no doubt that some records of rarities will have 'slipped through the net' – but the following list will give a good general overview of the status of the vast majority of species.

Red-throated Diver
An occasional winter visitor to coastal sites, being seen at least annually, most often off coasts of Cataluña.

Black-throated Diver
Much more regular in its occurrence than the last species, turning up in most years off the coasts of Valencia and Cataluña. More regular off the coasts of Cataluña, where it is regular off some headlands.

Great Northern Diver
A very scarce and irregular winter vagrant, which currently appears to be turning up more regularly.

Little Grebe
A numerous breeding resident of suitable wetland sites throughout the region, with, for example, 50-80 pairs breeding on El Hondo in most years, and undoubtedly more on the Albufera de Valencia and the Ebro Delta. Winter numbers much higher, with quite large flocks building up on open waters throughout.

Great Crested Grebe
A very common winter visitor to coastal and wetland sites throughout the region. In the breeding season, takes up territory on most suitable waters, though density varies according to disturbance, etc. A recent census found some 70 pairs on the Albufera de Valencia.

Slavonian Grebe
A rare autumn and winter visitor, with records, often at intervals of several years, at coastal and wetland sites, with a tendency to greater frequency in recent years.

Red-necked Grebe
A few records exist for this species in Cataluña, always in autumn or winter.

Black-necked Grebe
A characteristic wintering species of coastal and wetland sites throughout, with the laguna de La Mata often hosting flocks in excess of 2,000 birds. Breeds sparingly on El Hondo, where it had increased in recent years, to a level of 90 pairs in 1997, and at the Albufera.

Cory's Shearwater
A breeding species of the Columbretes Islands, and possibly of one or two other islets. It is, however, likely that many of the birds seen moving along the coasts of our region in spring and autumn, and following fishing boats throughout the warmer months, refer to the Balearic Islands' considerable populations. Can be seen at any season, but particularly in the warmer months.

Great Shearwater
There are some four records of this species off Catalan coasts to date, and a June 1996 observation may point to a young bird 'wintering' (Southern Hemisphere winter) in the Mediterranean.

Mediterranean Shearwater

Although this species may breed at a coastal location here and there, it seems likely that most of the often huge flocks seen offshore, hail from the Balearics. In early spring, as many as a thousand birds per hour may pass headlands at many points on the coast. In winter, virtually the entire population of the subspecies *mauretanicus* seems to be concentrated along our coast, where the fishing is relatively productive. The subspecific complications of the species, involving more easterly populations, are better dealt with in the appropriate literature.

Storm Petrel

A breeding species on offshore islets, certainly including the Columbretes, Benidorm Island, the Medes islands, off the coast of Girona, and Tabarca, but its nocturnal habits mean it is seldom seen from shore.

Swinhoe's Storm Petrel

A subadult male was caught and ringed on Benidorm Island on 13th July, 1994.

Gannet

A common wintering species off all coasts, usually from September to April. A bird caught by fishermen off Santa Pola in 1994 had been ringed as a chick in a colony in the Channel Islands.

Masked Booby

On was seen off Valencia in March, 1989.

Cormorant

A common winter visitor in often very large numbers, to wetland and coastal sites, where it is much resented by fishermen. Breeding now occurs in Northern Spain, and it is not impossible that this species will colonise the region in the future. Many wintering birds show the white underparts of the *sinensis* and *maroccanus* races.

Shag

Breeds (or has bred) on the Columbretes, and probably in very low numbers on the coast of Alicante. Slightly more numerous in Cataluña, where a recent survey recorded about 10 pairs on the rocky headlands and islets there. Records further south, are, however, very scarce, though a few are seen each winter in the area of the Peñon de Ifach, Calpe and Tabarca.

Bittern

A scarce breeding species of Aiguamolls (6 pairs) and the Ebro Delta (4 pairs), with occasional records of breeding attempts elsewhere, most recently at El Hondo, where may have bred in recent summers.

Little Bittern

Common breeding visitor to suitable coastal wetlands throughout, with a very few birds staying on to winter. Densities vary, but recent census results have shown, for example, at least 100 pairs for the Albufera de Valencia alone, and it is one of the characteristic birds of the region's larger reedbeds.

Night Heron

Basically a summer visitor, present from March through to late autumn, but scarce, secretive and local. A few do stay to winter, mainly in the warm southern areas. Perhaps most likely to be seen near traditional daytime roosts, which it may well share with Cattle Egrets and other herons, though one such, near La Marina, Alicante, is in mature pines well away from water. Also nests colonially, with important populations in the Ebro Delta (170 pairs), the Albufera (320) pairs at a recent count) and El Hondo/Santa Pola (84 pairs).

Squacco Heron
An fairly common, but always local, summer visitor, very occasionally leaving a few juveniles behind to winter, at the major wetland sites throughout the coastal areas from the Ebro (450 pairs) southwards. Normally present from early April to early October. May be on the increase in our area.

Cattle Egret
A success-story in recent years, this species is on the increase throughout the region, wherever livestock or irrigated fields are the norm. Has increased, for example, from zero to some 1350 pairs, in the El Hondo/Santa Pola area, in less than ten years, whilst the Albufera probably holds three times that number. A year-round resident, often associating with Jackdaws.

Little Egret
Common, if local, at all wetland sites, the population augmented by wintering birds from further north each autumn.Around a thousand pairs breed on the Albufera, but numbers at El Hondo, for instance, depend heavily on seasonal water-level fluctuations.

Western Reef Heron
An occasional vagrant, to be found amongst flocks of the previous species, when care should be exercised due to the possibility of the rare grey form of Little Egret. In recent years, a pair has been found breeding on the Albufera de Valencia.

Great White Egret
Recently found breeding first in the Camargue, Southern France, and now in wetlands to the north of our area, it should only be a matter of time before this species becomes a regular breeder, instead of its current status as an occasional winter visitor, to be hoped for at any wetland area, and regular in the Ebro Delta.

Grey Heron
A breeding resident, especially of the Albufera and Ebro Delta sites, and abundant winter visitor, building up some impressive flocks at that season, when, for example, counts can be well in excess of 1,000 birds at the Albufera, and several hundred at Santa Pola.

Purple Heron
This largely solitary heron is a summer visitor, from early April until early October, breeding sparingly at most wetland sites.

Black Stork
A casual but steadily increasing migrant, whose occurences tend to be at least annual, and most often in the months of September and October, when its unmistakeable appearance means that it is seldom overlooked. 39 individuals were seen passing through Cataluña in 1996.

White Stork
March and September are the favourite months for sightings of this species in southern areas, when singletons and small groups are often seen heading along mountain ridges, or pausing to feed in lowland fields. They can, however, appear at almost any time of year. A very small breeding population (24 pairs in 1998) exists near the coast of Girona Province, and other pairs breed in villages of Zaragoza, close to the borders of Teruel. Small groups are also found wintering at, for example, Aiguamolls.

Glossy Ibis
Started to breed in the Albufera de Valencia in 1993, and successful breeding has taken place annually since then. Also bred in the Ebro Delta in 1996 (4 pairs) and at El Hondo/Santa Pola, where young have been raised in 1997 and 1998. Small groups are now regular at most wetland sites, and double figures are not unusual at the main marshes.

Spoonbill
An irregular migrant to many coastal and wetland sites, often turning up, in small groups, during March or September, and sometimes remaining at a site for several days. Winter records also exist.

Greater Flamingo
This emblematic species, whose conservation presents considerable problems, due not least to its requirements in terms of undisturbed saltmarsh, now breeds, though not every year, at three sites within the region, El Hondo, where up to 600 pairs have bred in recent years, the Ebro Delta (1500 pairs), and, in 1999, 2000 at Pétrola, where a few pairs may have raised young in a new colony. Disturbance has recently prevented breeding at Santa Pola, where success was last met with in the fifties. Big non-breeding populations are to be seen at many sites, most notably – and visibly – at Santa Pola, where winter flocks of up to 2,000 are not unusual. Major threats include power-lines, over-flying light aircraft and the ingestion of quantities of lead-shot picked up from the bottom of over-hunted waters.

Lesser Flamingo
Occasional individuals are reported amongst flocks of the last species. The possibility, at least, of their being genuinely wild birds cannot be overlooked in this area.

Mute Swan
Present in small numbers at Aiguamolls, where they originated from captive stock, and occasionally seen in the Ebro Delta.

Bewick's Swan
There have been three or four records of this northern vagrant, at different wetlands, in the last ten years.

Whooper Swan
The first record for Cataluña was of a second-year bird, in the Ebro Delta, in November 1994.

Bean Goose
An individual was seen at El Hondo in mid-December, 1997. Occurs occasionally further north, but nowhere with regularity.

Grey Lag Goose
A regular winter visitor to wetland sites, notably the Ebro Delta. Groups of up to 30 are not uncommon, here and at El Hondo/Santa Pola. Reports of other grey geese are always 'on' – especially when winters further north are hard.

Ruddy Shelduck
Odd birds – and occasionally, parties of three or four – turn up in concentrations of the next species, especially in the south of Alicante, though may be met with almost anywhere. The provenance of 'wildness' is, of course, an impossible issue, as with other wildfowl.

Shelduck
A species gradually extending its range, probably from the south of France. First bred in the Ebro Delta in about 1972, and at El Hondo in 1986, and now breeding at several sites, especially in the south of Alicante. Winter concentrations build up as high as up to 300 individuals at Santa Pola.

Wigeon
A moderate winter visitor, with some big flocks appearing on the open waters of the Ebro (13,700 in a recent survey), Albufera and El Hondo, as well as at inland sites like Pétrola. As with other wildfowl, numbers vary from year to year. A count of 772 on the Albufera in 1994 was notable.

Gadwall
A scarce breeding species in very small numbers at wetland sites, especially the Ebro Delta (some 300 pairs). A winter census on the Albufera usually reveals counts in three figures, but elsewhere always fairly sparsely represented.

Teal
Common, if local, winter visitor and passage migrant. A species which often responds to hunting pressures by keeping out of sight. Numbers in the Delta del Ebro have reached 18500 in good winters. May have bred in very small numbers at Aiguamolls.

Mallard
Common breeding species and winter visitor to all suitable waters. Winter counts may realise over 600 birds at Santa Pola, a staggering 42, 800 in the Ebro Delta, and a good autumn census saw some 5,500 birds on the Albufera in 1993. Breeding numbers are much lower, of course, with an estimated 200 pairs at El Hondo, for example.

Black Duck
An individual of this species was found at the Llobregat Delta in November 1996, which, if accepted, will be the third Spanish record.

Pintail
A winter visitor in highly variable numbers, depending upon hunting pressures. May reach thousands on the Ebro and at the Albufera.

Garganey
Passage migrant, especially in March, when good flocks may be found passing through. Also stays to breed in small numbers on wetlands, mainly in the northern part of the region, though occasionally as far south as El Hondo.

Blue-winged Teal
Two ringing recoveries, each of birds marked in Canada, are on record for Santa Pola (1969 & 1971) There are also three Catalan records, the most recent being from Aiguamolls in April 1996.

Shoveler
Abundant winter visitor, reaching numbers of several thousand on larger waters (20,000 on the Ebro Delta, and 28,000 on the Albufera). Breeds in very small numbers at suitable sites.

Marbled Duck
Although a few winter each year at El Hondo, this species is overwhelmingly a summer breeding visitor, now increasing rapidly from a position of great vulnerability a few years ago. (An estimated 90 individuals in 1993) Now breeding as far north as the Marjal del Moro, and a recent census counted over 750 birds at El Hondo (July 1998), still this bird's European stronghold. In 1997, some 96 pairs bred there. Water-levels have to be maintained to ensure the species' survival. A shy and retiring bird, it is often easiest to see in the post-breeding months, when small flocks gather on open water. Two records from Cataluña in 1996 give hope of range-extension.

Red-crested Pochard
Winter counts at all the major wetland sites are normally healthy, with numbers approaching the 11,000 mark at the Albufera. As a breeding species, however, more local and sparsely-distributed. Not found breeding on northernmost waters of the region, but represented at all suitable sites from the Ebro (2.000 pairs) southwards.

Pochard
Abundant winter visitor and local breeding species, preferring smaller pools in summer. may reach close to 15,000 birds in some winters, on larger stretches of water, such as found in the Ebro Delta.

Ferruginous Duck
Normally found in the region only as a scarce winter vagrant, often amongst flocks of the previous species, and on larger waters, like the Albufera, where it is annual. Has bred from time to time, including a pair which raised eight young at the Clot de Galvany in 1990, and a possible breeding record at the Albufera in 1994.

Tufted Duck
Winter visitor in small numbers to all suitable waters, seldom reaching three figures, except on the Albufera, and perhaps on the Ebro Delta.

Scaup
A very rare winter visitor, occuring just about annually, usually with Pochard flocks.

Eider
A rare winter vagrant, most often recorded off the Ebro Delta, but with records from most coastal sites.

Common Scoter
Small flocks pass along the coast each winter, December and January being the usual months. Numbers appear to increase to the north of the region.

Velvet Scoter
Much rarer in the south than the previous species, but has appeared offshore at least once, off Valencia, in 1989, and there is an odd record of two, on an Elche reservoir(!), in January 1985. Off Cataluña, more frequent, and regular in the Bay of Rosas.

Goldeneye
Turns up occasionally on the larger waters in winter, but records are scarce, and certainly less than annual. In common with other scarce wildfowl, both listed here and otherwise, could be worth seeking during spells of cold weather further north.

Smew
Very rare winter wanderer to Cataluña.

Red-breasted Merganser
A winter visitor in small numbers, along rocky shores anywhere.

Goosander
Rare winter vagrant to northerly parts of the region.

Ruddy Duck
Sufficient has been written elsewhere about this intrusive interloper from North America (via Slimbridge!). Suffice to say that records are increasing, and the threat to the population of the next species is both real and, possibly, inevitable. Difficulty in identification of females, and especially hybrids, complicates the issue.

White-headed Duck
The Spanish population of this delightful little duck was down to an all-time low of 22 birds in 1977, so that a total of 617 individuals found during a census of El Hondo in early 1999 represents a huge and welcome increase at this, the species' new stronghold. Records further north are still scarce, but increasing. The threat of interbreeding by the previous species is the one great shadow over this increase, and it is hoped that control measures will have at least some effect in maintaining the purity of the species.

Honey Buzzard
Breeds sparingly in the far north of our region, in the woodlands of Girona Province. Further south, met with as a passage migrant, usually during a period of strong westerlies, typically in mid-May or late September.

Black-shouldered Kite
Perhaps a future colonist of the region, the only records are of one at a site in the northwest of Valencia Province in 1992, one at Pétrola in February 1999, another at El Hondo in October of that year, and three old records for Cataluña, where at least two more were found in 1996. Increasing steadily in its strongholds further west, however, and worth keeping an eye out for!

Black Kite
Has bred around Barcelona, and may do so in the extreme west of Valencia and Teruel, but much more likely to be seen as a passage migrant, when small numbers pass annually along mountain ridges and coasts.

Red Kite
Scarcer than the last species. Breeds in very small numbers close to the French border, in hilly woodland, but elsewhere a wanderer.

Lammergeier
A recent report of one over a sierra in the south of Alicante almost certainly refers to the captive-breeding and release programme aimed at re-introducing the species to the Sierra de Cazorla, away to the southwest of our region, in Jaén Province. Breeds, of course, in the foothills of the Catalán Pyrenees, covered by the Pyrenean guidebook.

Egyptian Vulture
Represented in our region by a small breeding population in the Maestrazgo and Teruel Province. Elsewhere a scarce migrant.

Griffon Vulture
Breeds in the rocky canyons associated with tributaries of the Ebro, and is common around Gallocanta, for example. Otherwise, sightings are of itinerant groups in autumn and winter, when as many as 200 birds have been seen in parties, wandering far and wide. Mountainous areas and coastal plains are visited in most years, and throughout the region.

Black Vulture
This rare and threatened species has been recorded in several recent winters. A bird seen around Orihuela in the winter of 1996-7 had been colour-marked in a release-programme in southern France, from whence another individual strayed to Llobregat in the same winter.

Short-toed Eagle
A scarce and local breeding species, restricted to quiet, wooded mountains throughout the region. Also a passage migrant, arriving sometimes as early as February, with the return passage usually in September and October.

Marsh Harrier
Sparse breeder at the more northerly wetlands (for instance 14 pairs at Aiguamolls), passage migrant, and common winter visitor. Some sizeable roosts can build up during the winter months, at sites like the Albufera and El Hondo, where some 50 females/young birds are the norm, with adult males comparatively rare.

Hen Harrier
Winter visitor in small numbers to marshes and upland plains.

Montagu's Harrier
Breeds around the most extensive coastal marshlands throughout the region, and passes through on both passages. Breeding densities are normally quite low, but the Castellón Province census of 1994 showed between 50 and 60 pairs breeding. First arrivals are in late March or early April, and most birds have gone by late September.

Goshawk
A tough one, this. Breeds widely, throughout the entire area of this guide, but its secretive and sedentary habits give little chance of a casual sighting, except perhaps in wnter, when a few descend from their montane woodlands to feed on coastal wetlands. Perhaps the best breeding areas are the upland woods of Cataluña, basically the pre-Pyrenean ranges, and similar areas in Teruel and the Maestrazgo region.

Sparrowhawk
More likely to be found wintering in the lowlands than the last species, when many may be birds from Northern Europe. Otherwise found in much the same habitats as the Goshawk, but usually more likely to be seen.

Buzzard
Locally common breeding bird, anywhere in suitable habitat, but relatively abundant as a winter visitor, frequenting many habitat-types. Many birds show characters of the various (and variable) paler colour-forms, found typically in northeast Europe.

Long-legged Buzzard
A singleton appeared at El Hondo on similar dates in late November, in 1995 and 1996, and in March 1997. Not uncommon just a short distance away in North Africa.

Rough-legged Buzzard
One was seen at the Marjal del Moro in January 1993, and there are infrequent records further north, including two in Cataluña in 1996. This, and other, irruptive species can be confidently expected in the future, with the growth of observer-competence.

Spotted Eagle
A small rash of records occurred in the winters of the early 1990's, at El Hondo, with two birds present in at least one winter, but none recorded there since 1993. At the Ebro Delta, singles occurred in two winters in the nineties. As this eastern species winters in the Camargue, South of France, with some regularity, it is always 'on the cards.'

Golden Eagle
A sedentary breeding resident of much of the region's mountainous interior, it is always scarce away from known breeding areas.

Booted Eagle
A locally common summer visitor to wooded hill country in Castellón, rarer in Alicante. Regular on both passages almost anywhere, and common as a winter visitor to the coastal wetlands. At El Hondo/Santa Pola, for example, between ten and fifteen individuals normally winter, pale phase birds forming the great majority.

Bonelli's Eagle
Locally common breeding resident, seldom straying far from breeding cliffs, although post-breeding dispersal accounts for the wanderings of dark juveniles, which can turn up in many places. There may be as many as 200 pairs in the region, and breeding normally takes place quite early in the year, the young being fledged by mid-May. A species under threat from hunting and other pressures.

Osprey
Winter visitor in good numbers to all wetland areas, and common passage migrant. Undoubtedly once bred, and may do so again if encouraged. A ring from a Scottish-bred bird has been read at Santa Pola. 32 individuals passed over Barcelona in autumn 1996.

Lesser Kestrel
An unpredictable breeding bird in the region. Colonies have been formed at widely-spaced sites, and often abandoned immediately, or after only one year. An introduction programme is currently being carried out in the north of Alicante Province – there seems to be little reason for the species' scarcity, compared to similar sites in Extremadura, for example. There exists a notable stronghold of this species, breeding in the abandoned farmhouses of Los Monegros, just outside our area, in Zaragoza Province. (see 'A birdwatching Guide to the Pyrenees')

Kestrel
A common breeding resident throughout.

Red-footed Falcon
Recent springs have seen a batch of observations, in line with those recorded in France and Great Britain, though there are never more than a scattering of records, usually from well-watched sites!

Merlin
Regular winter visitor to sites offering plenty of small birds, such as El Hondo and the Ebro Delta. Usually seen singly.

Hobby
Very scarce breeding bird in suitable country, and fairly common passage migrant, usually in October, when individuals often stay around for some time at favoured locations. Most common in the Ebro valley.

Eleonora's Falcon
Some thirty pairs breed on the Columbretes. At wetland sites along the coast, occurs with some regularity, usually in autumn.

Lanner Falcon
One at the Ebro Delta, in January 1996, may well have been a wild bird, and showed characters of the North African race. A juvenile was at Llobregat the following June.

Peregrine
Breeding resident at suitable cliffs, both montane and coastal, throughout. Also a winter visitor to wetland sites.

Red-legged Partridge
A common resident throughout the region, hunted extensively everywhere.

Quail
A common summer visitor to cereal fields everywhere. A few overwinter.

Pheasant
Resident in the woods of Cataluña (Barcelona and Girona Provinces) Occasional elsewhere, some birds being released for shooting.

Water Rail
A common – if frequently overlooked – resident of all wetland areas.

Spotted Crake
Breeds at the Marjal del Moro (probably up to 3 pairs) and possibly elsewhere, though certainly scarce. More often met with on passage, and may also overwinter occasionally. As with other species of this family, study is very difficult.

Little Crake
A scarce breeding visitor to Aiguamolls, and probably one or two other sites along the coast, though isolated winter and early spring (February to April) records are not infrequent.

Baillon's Crake
Probably marginally commoner than the last species, and certainly breeds at several coastal wetlands, most notably at the Ebro Delta (50 pairs), but probably under-recorded, due to its extreme stealth.

Corn Crake
Formerly bred in Lleida (Lerida) Province, just to the west of our area, and may still do so. Otherwise an unlikely but possible passage migrant just about anywhere.

Moorhen
A common resident at all suitable wetlands and many riverine sites throughout the region.

Purple Gallinule
A species enjoying a current range-expansion, after a crash in about the nineteen-fifties, and now breeding at sites along the whole length of the coast, wherever there are suitable reedbeds. May be difficult to find during the breeding season, but can be almost confiding at other seasons. Densities vary, but the best places to find this sought-after species are the Marjal del Moro (18 pairs in 1996 and increasing rapidly) and Aiguamolls (35 pairs).

Coot
Common breeding resident at all suitable waters, passage migrant and abundant winter visitor.

Red-knobbed Coot
This extreme rarity has turned up with some regularity at El Hondo/Santa Pola in recent winters. Bred at El Hondo in 1993, when drought meant that the young had to be brought to Valencia and reared artificially. Since then, has been seen from time to time at the same site. Has a very small 'base' in Cádiz Province, and the entire Spanish population probably does not exceed 25 pairs Has been found recently breeding at the Marjal del Moro, and may well be worth seeking there.

Common Crane
A regular migrant and winter visitor, irregular in character, except at Gallocanta, where big numbers (for example, 54,000 in November 1989) can turn up in late autumn. Their occurrence there, however, depends upon several factors, principally water levels at that site, but also prevailing conditions elsewhere on their route.

Demoiselle Crane
A singleton was with a party of the last species at Gallocanta, at the end of 1996.

Little Bustard
Found as a breeding species in the neighbourhood of Gallocanta, as well as around Pétrola, and at other sites close to the borders of Alicante with Valencia and Albacete. Always scarce, but apt to wander outside the breeding season, when can be met with almost anywhere, particularly in cereal crops and on saline flats.

Great Bustard
Breeds in fair numbers at Pétrola and at other points in Albacete Province, as well as in the Gallocanta area. Like the last species, tends to wander outside the nesting season, when its conspicuous size render it easy to find. May be increasing slightly now that it enjoys complete protection, but still vulnerable to furtive hunting and habitat-loss.

Oystercatcher
Breeds in the Ebro Delta, where it seems to increasing slowly, but still with less than fifty pairs, at the time of writing. Elsewhere, a scarce passage migrant and winter visitor to coastal sites.

Black-winged Stilt
An abundant and conspicuous breeding species at all coastal and inland wetlands. Passage is common in spring and autumn, but the population thins out notably in winter, when Stilts tend to disappear from some of their colder and less sheltered haunts. Census results bear out these impressions.

Avocet
Common visitor to many wetlands, but breeding is normally restricted to big colonies at the Ebro Delta and Santa Pola, where some 500 pairs breed, and a few much smaller groups, many of which appear to be temporary, and depend on factors such as water-levels, especially on endorreic lagoons like Pétrola. Also a passage migrant and abundant winter visitor to most coastal sites.

Stone Curlew
Breeds on stony plains throughout the region, but may also be met with on passage. has important wintering areas around la Mata, when concentrations may number up to 300 birds. Often best located by listening for the song at dusk, during the breeding season.

Cream-coloured Courser
This saharan species has occurred in Albacete, and could be a candidate for vagrancy, so close to the African coast.

Collared Pratincole
Breeds sparingly at coastal wetlands, arriving in late March, and staying into September. A vulnerable species, due to its preferred exposed nest-sites in fields and saltmarshes, which can be affected by disturbance from people, dogs, cats, foxes, and even rain. 99 pairs have been counted in the Ebro Delta, and up to 50 pairs in the Santa Pola/el Hondo area.

Little Ringed Plover
Widely distributed as a breeding species at suitably stony freshwater shores, banks and gravel-pits throughout, but never very numerous in summer. Common on both passages, and occasionally overwinters.

Ringed Plover
A common passage bird and winter visitor at all wetlands.

Kentish Plover
A common breeding species at all coastal wetlands, as well as many inland saline lagoons, and some man-made sites such a gravel-workings. Breeding densities can often be quite high, as evidence the 1700 pairs in the Ebro Delta, and 160 pairs recently recorded at La Mata. Present all year.

Greater Sand Plover
A juvenile was found in the Ebro Delta in August 1996.

Dotterel
A scarce migrant, to be looked for on either passage, most often on bare coastal fields, where odd winter sightings have also been made. Up to 13 birds were present throughout virtually the whole of September, 1999, at El Hondo.

Pacific Golden Plover
A March 1996 record from the Ebro Delta has been submitted to the rarities committee. If accepted, it will be the first record for the region, and the second for Spain.

Golden Plover
A regular winter visitor, flocks seldom exceeding 100 birds, to many agricultural and saltmarsh areas.

Grey Plover
Winter visitor and passage migrant in small numbers to all coastal and some inland waters.

Lapwing
A few pairs breed at one or two isolated coastal sites, and. more numerously, at Pétrola. Otherwise a common winter visitor, especially to the rice-fields of the Ebro Delta and Albufera, for example, where flocks may reach four figures. Scarcer further south.

Red Knot
A scarce migrant through the region, most often appearing in May and, on return passage, in September, though seldom in large numbers – most records are of ones and twos.

Sanderling
Common winter visitor to many coastal sites and beaches. Also regular on both passages.

Semipalmated Sandpiper
One was at the Delta de Llobregat in June 1997.

Little Stint
Abundant in winter and on passage at all suitable wetlands.

Temminck's Stint
Scarce but regular passage bird and occasional winter visitor to freshwater marshes throughout. Probably most numerous in April and July.

Least Sandpiper
August 1996 provided the second Spanish record for this American – at the Ebro Delta.

White-rumped Sandpiper
There have been two records of this American vagrant in Valencia, the more recent being in July 1994, at the Albufera.

Pectoral Sandpiper
A scattering of records of this species in Valencia and Cataluña in the early 1990's probably suggests under-recording of this Asiatic/North American wanderer, which has since become almost annual.

Curlew Sandpiper
Common passage migrant, often in impressive flocks (over 1,000 birds at Santa Pola on several recent autumn passages).

Purple Sandpiper
A very rare winter visitor to rocky coastlines, by no means annual, and usually accompanying Sanderling and/or Turnstone.

Dunlin
Abundant winter visitor and passage migrant.(21000 in the Ebro Delta in winter)

Broad-billed Sandpiper
There is one June record (1992) of this species at Santa Pola, which has also been seen some four times in the nineties in Cataluña, though not annually.

Buff-breasted Sandpiper
There have been several recent autumn records of this rare visitor from Eastern Asia or North America, so far only in Valencia and Cataluña.

Ruff
A scarce winter visitor and common migrant to suitable sites. Many hundreds are liable to appear in April, especially at sites like Pétrola. Less numerous on return passage.

Jack Snipe
A very scarce winter visitor, commoner in northern areas, such as Aiguamolls, where 20 individuals were recently counted. A slight increase in March records tends to indicate a small spring passage in that month.

Snipe
Regular winter visitor and passage migrant to most suitable marshes. Possibly breeds in the Ebro Delta, but proof is not forthcoming.

Great Snipe
There are, to date, some thirteen records for the region of this elusive Eastern vagrant.

Long-billed Dowitcher
One was seen at the Llobregat Delta in late autumn 1998. Other unconfirmed records exist.

Woodcock
Breeds sparingly in the woodlands of Cataluña. Elsewhere a scarce winter visitor to coastal sites, and occasionally to poplar plantations inland.

Black-tailed Godwit
A very common passage migrant and abundant winter visitor, especially to the southern sites, where flocks may reach several hundred. 4,600 have been recorded in winter in the Ebro, but more than 10,000 there on passage.

Bar-tailed Godwit
Scarce migrant, mainly in autumn, though there are regular records in May. Never very numerous, and usually at coastal sites, though a maximum of 500 winter in the Ebro, varying a great deal from year to year.

Whimbrel
A common passage migrant on both journeys, and occasional winter visitor, especially to the south of the region.

Curlew
Slightly more common in winter than the previous species, but never numerous, and scarcer on passage than its relative.

Spotted Redshank
Winters commonly in the south of Alicante and in the Ebro Delta, and is a familiar passage migrant throughout the region.

Redshank
Breeds at most wetlands along the coast of Valencia, Castellón and Tarragona. Elsewhere a common passage migrant and winter visitor.

Marsh Sandpiper
Annual in spring, usually in March and April, when it can be seen on almost any freshwater marsh. Winter records are scarce, but do occur. Autumn birds are less frequent than spring sightings.

Greenshank
Common passage migrant at both seasons, and scarce wintering species, especially to southern sites.

Lesser Yellowlegs
A mid-July record from the Albufera, in 1994, of a first-year bird, was the first of some twelve Spanish records which was not in spring or autumn. A juvenile was also seen in the Ebro Delta in November 1996, and a bird was seen at El Hondo in September 1999. A vagrant from North America.

Green Sandpiper
Sparingly distributed in winter, and only slightly more common as a passage migrant, most often met with in March.

Wood Sandpiper
Locally distributed in winter, but common as a passage migrant, the largest flocks tending to be in April, at suitable, usually freshwater marshes.

Terek Sandpiper
A considerable rarity anywhere in Spain, this eastern species has been recorded twice in the Valencian Community in recent years, the later being one at Santa Pola in August 1993. More frequent in Cataluña, where it has recently appeared annually, including an overwintering juvenile in th Ebro Delta in 1995-6.

Common Sandpiper
Breeds at suitable, often riverine, localities in the northern half of our region. Otherwise a familiar passage migrant and winter visitor.

Turnstone
Common passage migrant, mainly along the coast. Can be seen at most seasons, but wintering is largely restricted to the southern half of the region.

Wilson's Phalarope
A female was at Santa Pola in May 1987. This nearctic species is always a candidate for vagrancy.

Red-necked Phalarope
Scarce and erratic migrant, most often seen in May and September, normally singly, though there is a December (1989) record of two birds at Santa Pola, whilst a group of 8 was in the Ebro Delta in September 1996.

Grey Phalarope
Scarce and even more erratic in pattern of occurrence than the previous species, usually located after autumnal gales, in coastal lagoons. Also occasional in winter.

Pomarine Skua
Most years see just a few records, in spring and autumn, of this rare coastal wanderer.

Arctic Skua
An erratic but regular spring and autumn migrant along the coast, usually seen pursuing gulls and terns. Occasional in winter.

Long-tailed Skua
The rarest of the skuas, as one might expect, and certainly less than annual, most records being in May, though a bird was seen in December 1992, with a group of Black-headed Gulls, near Valencia.

Great Skua
Rare migrant and winter visitor. A Shetland-ringed bird was recovered at Santa Pola in July 1976.

Mediterranean Gull
A species whose presence seems to be reduced, compared to previous abundance, at least in the southern part of the region. Still common in winter along the more northerly coasts, where January numbers can be impressive (16000 examples in the Ebro). Has bred irregularly in the Ebro Delta since 1987, and occasionally at Santa Pola in recent years.

Laughing Gull
An immature was seen at Santa Pola in October 1993. There is also a July 1988 record for the Ebro Delta.

Little Gull
Another species much reduced from previous relatively common status, and winter flocks seem now to be a thing of the past. Typically occurs in ones and twos in April and May, at coastal wetlands. In April 1996, a group of 450 birds was seen at sea, some 9 miles off Barcelona.

Sabine's Gull
One was seen in Santa Pola harbour in September 1997, the first record since 1992, when nearby El Pinet was the venue for a March sighting.

Black-headed Gull
Breeds at several coastal sites, and winters widely, sometimes in huge numbers (e.g. 58,000 censused at the Albufera in January 1997.)

Slender-billed Gull
A rapid increase is taking place in this species' breeding status along the coast, where saline lagoons are its favoured habitat. In the Ebro Delta, some 600 pairs were breeding in 1996, after first colonising the area in 1980. Outside the Ebro Delta, Santa Pola has the largest population, with post-breeding flocks currently around 400 birds. Can now be seen, however, at all favourable sites, and may well soon breed at virtually all of them.

Audouin's Gull
Breeds on the Columbretes Islands (latest census some 275 pairs on the Illa Grossa) and in the Ebro Delta, where some 11,000 pairs probably constitute this species' major breeding site worldwide. The coast of the region is one of the best places in the world to observe this local gull, and post-nuptial flocks can attain numbers of over 500 at Santa Pola, as well as perhaps 200 at nearby La Mata. Present throughout the year, but entirely coastal in distribution, only crossing land to roost on salt-lakes. A recent fishing moratorium caused a sudden and rapid decline, however, and the situation must be watched.

Ring-billed Gull
A couple of recent sightings on the Albufera de Valencia (one in Oct/Nov 1992, another in July/August 1994) are unsurprising in view of this bird's increasing tendency to wander to Europe.

Common Gull
Common, it isn't! Most years see just an odd record of this northern gull, at widely-separated coastal sites.

Lesser Black-backed Gull
Around 120 pairs breed in the Ebro Delta, but otherwise, this species is known as a common winter visitor to the coast.

Yellow-legged Gull
An all-too-numerous breeding species at most coastal sites and islets, predating colonies of most seabirds, and forming huge flocks at rubbish tips.

Herring Gull
The sole reliable record of this northern species is of a female in the Ebro Delta, in April 1996. Please note that the identification of this species must be ascertained using criteria other than simply leg-colour, due to variability in this character of the previous species.

Iceland Gull
Two birds were present at Santa Pola for most of May 1994.

Great Black-backed Gull
A considerable rarity, with a bias, curiously, towards occurrence in August, almost always singly, and at various coastal sites.

Kittiwake
Restricted to winter sightings, usually after strong winds, and at various coastal locations. A record for April 1994, off Castellón, was highly unusual.

Gull-billed Tern
A highly localised and scarce breeding species and passage migrant. The Albufera and the Ebro Delta (300 pairs) are the best coastal locations, but regular breeding takes place in the Pétrola and Gallocanta areas, when water-levels permit. More numerous as a breeding species somewhat to the west of our region, on favoured lagoons of Castilla-La Mancha.

Caspian Tern
An irregular visitor to coasts, occurring in virtually any month of the year, at coastal locations, usually in ones and twos. The best months for records tend to be March, April and July. Has bred in the Ebro Delta, and may well do so again.

Lesser Crested Tern
Now breeding in very small numbers in the Ebro Delta, and has interbred (1994) with the next species at the Albufera. Otherwise most likely to be seen as an autumn vagrant, often with flocks of the next species.

Sandwich Tern
Breeds at The Ebro Delta (1900 pairs), the Albufera de Valencia, and, when left un-molested, at Santa Pola. Otherwise an abundant passage migrant and winter visitor in small numbers to coastal sites.

Common Tern
Passage migrant along the coast in huge numbers, the spring movement starting at the end of March. Breeds in good numbers at the Ebro Delta (5,000 pairs), the Albufera (1,600 pairs) and, more sparingly, in the south of Alicante. Winter records are extremely scarce.

Arctic Tern
An observation at Santa Pola in September 1990 was a surprise.

Royal Tern
There are just two records from Santa Pola in September of this vagrant.

Little Tern
Local breeding species, best represented at the Ebro Delta (some 500 pairs), and at the Albufera and Santa Pola (each with some 200 pairs). Also passage migrant, mainly in April and August/September.

Whiskered Tern
A vulnerable species, reduced from former levels by drought and habitat-loss, but still common as a breeding bird in the south of Alicante, at the Albufera and in the Ebro Delta. A few overwinter from time to time in the south of the region.

Black Tern
Now almost entirely a migrant through the region, most likely to be seen in easterly winds in April/May and in September or October. Has bred at several sites and may yet do so again, but is now much reduced throughout Spain.

White-winged Black Tern
A typical vagrant on easterly winds in May and sometimes in August/September, usually in small flocks to wetland sites.

Guillemot
Much scarcer than the next species – in fact a considerable rarity, with the last traceable records being of one in Santa Pola harbour in January 1985, and one on the beach of Tossa de Mar in June 1996.

Razorbill
A regular winter visitor to our coasts, highly variable in pattern of occurrence from one winter to the next.

Puffin
A rare vagrant, usually seen at sea or from coastal headlands in the winter months.

Black-bellied Sandgrouse
A local breeding species on salty and stony plains, such as around Gallocanta, where relatively common, and Pétrola (scarce).

Pin-tailed Sandgrouse
Scarcer than the last species, but definitely represented around Pétrola, and a few pairs inhabit the Gallocanta area. This and the previous species are clearly at much-reduced population-levels when compared to, say, the last century, before the loss of much natural habitat drove these sensitive birds into 'relic-habitats.'

Rock Dove
Yes, well . . .! Plenty of 'rock doves' are to be seen throughout. The presence of the odd black or white – or just about any other colour – bird may or may not put you off 'ticking' them.

Stock Dove
A local breeding species, probably more common than a casual glance may suggest. Winters on coastal fields, especially in Cataluña, Valencia and Castellón, sometimes in good flocks.

Woodpigeon
Common breeding species in all wooded areas, absent only from some lowland coastal areas. Numbers probably augmented in winter by flocks from the North.

Collared Dove (& Barbary Dove)
The former is a rapidly-increasing breeding resident wherever suitable habitats exist, mainly on the coast, but spreading inland. The presence of the escaped *risoria & rose-agriasea* forms has complicated the issue of identification, but it is the authors' impression that the vast majority of birds now breeding are actually colonising Collared Doves, which have invaded some areas with great rapidity.

Turtle Dove
A common breeding summer visitor to all suitable woodland throughout, arriving in late March, and leaving by early October.

Monk Parakeet
This escaped Argentinian guest has found Barcelona's parks and gardens much to its liking, and some 80% of the surprising Spanish population of some 500 pairs breed there. Also found around Valencia and in the south of Alicante.

Ring-necked Parakeet
Not as numerous as the previous species, this African and Asiatic 'escape' is nevertheless increasing, and may well be a pest of the future, especially around fruit-orchards. Most often seen around Alicante, Valencia and Barcelona.

N.B: Other species of parakeets, parrots and the like are by no means unusual, and the serious student of such matters will need to take care in the identification of any such 'exotica.'

Great Spotted Cuckoo
This rather elusive species is less so in the north of our region, where there is a denser population of Magpies, the principal 'host' of this summer visitor. March is the main arrival-month for the species, but February records are not unknown. The coastal strip, south of Barcelona, is largely avoided as a breeding area – host species are scarce here.

Cuckoo
Breeds throughout the region, frequenting many types of woodland and reedbed habitats. Exclusively a summer visitor, usually first appearing in March.

Barn Owl
A common breeding resident throughout, though its completely nocturnal lifestyle renders study difficult. Has a macabre liking for cemeteries.

Scops Owl
A common though local breeding summer visitor, nesting in holes in its favourite pine-woods, but also in the old nests of Magpies. May well be in decline in the region, but data are hard to come by due to the nocturnal habits of the species.

Eagle Owl
A common, though elusive, inhabitant of 'barrancos' (dry river-courses, often with steep sides, and, ideally, caves) wherever there is little disturbance, and rabbits. Present all year, but always under pressure from illegal hunting and nest-robbery. If you find a nest, keep it to yourself!

Little Owl
An abundant resident of many habitats throughout.

Tawny Owl
Common and widespread in Cataluña, less so as you move further south, but still present in the more extensive woodlands.

Long-eared Owl
Present and sedentary wherever there are dense pinewoods throughout the region.

Short-eared Owl
This species depends for its presence upon the cyclic population levels of the Common Vole, and, during 'plague years' of that mammal, has been found breeding in the lower Ebro valley. Otherwise, known as a scarce winter visitor, almost exclusively to coasts and coastal wetlands.

Nightjar
Generally commonest as a breeding species in the north of the area, frequenting the drier hillsides cloaked in 'matorral' (scrub), but occurs right down into Alicante, where it has recently been found breeding in close proximity to the next species.

Red-necked Nightjar
Common breeding visitor of warmer areas, preferring more mature woodland than the previous species. Arrives in April.

Common Swift
Abundant summer visitor to all parts, usually arriving in late March, the heaviest passage taking place in April, when many thousands pass through. Occasional winter sightings are recorded.

Pallid Swift
Arrives at its coastal strongholds earlier, on average, than the previous species, often by late February, and sometimes stays later at colonies, into October. As with the last species, winter records are not unknown. Normally breeds on sea-cliffs, but occasionally in buildings.

Alpine Swift
Common summer visitor and passage migrant, utilising cliffs and man-made structures like dams and walls for nesting. An early migrant, often arriving in February or early March.

Kingfisher
Common resident, but most birds retire from the coastal wetlands in summer, breeding in upland locations. Winter densities on the marshlands can be very high.

Bee Eater
Common summer visitor to all suitable sites. may be in decline, due to habitat-loss and agricultural change. Present or on passage from the end of March until October.

Roller
Scarce and declining summer visitor, threatened by changes in agricultural practice. Commonest in Girona and the Ebro valley. Late April is the best time for northward passage.

Hoopoe
Abundant summer visitor, passage migrant, and, in southern areas, winter visitor. Present in urban and suburban habitats, open woodland, and many types of agricultural area.

Wryneck

Wryneck
A fairly common but declining summer resident of woodland anywhere, but often difficult to detect when silent. Winters very sparingly in southern reedbeds.

Green Woodpecker
The Iberian race *Picus viridis sharpei* is a common year-round resident in woodland throughout, wandering to treeless wastes in winter, wherever there are ants.

Great Spotted Woodpecker
Only reaching down to the coast in northern Cataluña, this woodpecker is common in some inland areas, particularly the wooded valleys of Castellón and Teruel. Much harder to find in the south, and probably absent from Alicante Province.

Lesser Spotted Woodpecker
Has been recorded in inland areas of Castellón, and possibly Teruel. A few breeding pairs are quite possible, but this species is nowhere common in Spain, away from the north coast. A wanderer appeared at Aiguamolls in February 1996.

Dupont's Lark
This sought-after species breeds and is resident in the stony wastes of the areas south of Gallocanta, and at Moya, but its greatest stronghold is just outside the area covered by this guide, in the Ebro valley, and a visit to the plains of Belchite may well represent your best chance of finding the elusive bird. Several pairs do, however, inhabit the 'paramos' of Blanca. Familiarity with this bird's vocabulary is essential to its location!

Calandra Lark
A numerous breeding resident of much of Albacete, as well as the upland areas of Teruel. Forms sizeable flocks outside the breeding season.

Short-toed Lark
Summer visitor, with a preference for stony plains, and passage migrant, first arriving in late March.

Lesser Short-toed Lark
Year-round resident of saline flats and stony areas, usually with minimal vegetation. Tends to be southerly in distribution, commonest in the south of Alicante.

Crested Lark
An abundant resident of agricultural and waste land throughout, less likely to occur at higher altitudes than the next species, but often breeding virtually side-by-side, when familiarity with the species' respective vocabularies will help in their separation.

Thekla Lark
A common resident of stony uplands and coastal scrub throughout, though generally avoids agricultural lowlands.

Woodlark
Common though local resident of wooded mountains everywhere. Undertakes altitudinal migration in winter, when small flocks may be found in orchards and the like.

Skylark
Principally an abundant winter visitor to southern parts of the region, except to upland plains, where breeding occurs. Further north, breeds at lower levels, but is nowhere very numerous as a breeding species.

Sand Martin
Locally common breeding species and abundant passage migrant, first arriving in late February.
Winter records are not unknown.

Crag Martin
Breeds on suitable cliffs everywhere. In winter, descends to coastal marshes, where many hundreds may congregate, especially in gloomy weather.

Barn Swallow
Abundant summer visitor and passage migrant in huge numbers, starting the northward movement in late February, and passing southwards through to late October. Most years see a few winter records at southern localities, often caught up in flocks of Crag Martins.

Red-rumped Swallow
A local breeding species, most often found in the sub-Pyrenean areas of Girona, and in Castellón, but cropping up almost anywhere where bridges or abandoned houses provide breeding opportunities. Seems to be on the increase in southern parts of the region. First spring records may frequently be in February or early March.

House Martin
Abundant breeding visitor and passage migrant, whose presence from late February to November is occasionally extended throughout the winter, when very small numbers may be found with the Crag Martins in southern areas.

Richard's Pipit
Has been recorded in November on the Columbretes, and should be looked out for at coastal sites in late autumn.Two birds were at La Mata in December 1996, and one at Valencia, in February 1997, representing a departure from this species' normal pattern. (Or possibly improved observer-competence?)

Tawny Pipit
Sparsely-represented breeding visitor to bleak upland plains through the region, scarcer in the south, and probably in decline. Arrives in late March.

Tree Pipit
Breeds in wooded hills at the northern extremity of our region, and possibly the odd pair in the Sistema Ibérico. Otherwise a fairly common spring and autumn passage migrant.

Meadow Pipit
Abundant winter visitor to all suitable sites.

Red-throated Pipit
Scarce migrant, usually on easterly winds, in April and May, but annual, at least in recent years.
May be rarer in autumn, though this could be a reflection of its relative obscurity at that season!

Rock Pipit
The pattern of occurrence of this scarce visitor is no doubt complicated by its resemblance to the following species, with which it was once considered conspecific, but certainly appears in winter along the coast, sparingly.

Water Pipit
Common winter visitor in small numbers, to wetland areas throughout the region.

Yellow Wagtail
Common summer visitor to lowland areas, and passage migrant, present from February to October. Subspecific complications are too many for a volume of this size, but a 1999 April record, from Tabarca of a bird showing the characters of *M. f. feldegg*, which some authorities regard as a separate species, was a surprise. An example of the same race was found at the Delta de Llobregat in April 1994 – note the similar date.

Citrine Wagtail
This eastern vagrant has lately turned up with some regularity in the Ebro Delta, where no less than six examples have now been ringed. Spring and autumn appear to be similarly favoured, but a February bird, showing signs of moult, was seen in 1996. There have also been records at Aiguamolls.

Grey Wagtail
Common resident of clear streams, etc., through the region, and familiar passage migrant in October and March. Many also stay to winter in coastal areas.

White Wagtail
Winter visitor in great abundance, and breeding bird in much reduced numbers.

Dipper
Scarce breeding species in the mountains of Cataluña and the Sistema Ibérico.

Wren
Well-distributed breeding species of mountainous terrain throughout, dispersing into lowland areas in winter, but scarce near southern coasts.

Dunnock
Breeds in the north of Cataluña, as well as at high altitudes in the Sistema Ibérico. Elsewhere an erratic and scarce winter visitor.

Alpine Accentor
An erratic winter visitor to high ground and coastal sites, in small groups or singly.

Rufous Bush Robin
A scarce and secretive summer visitor, mainly to southern areas, largely restricted to Alicante, where it arrives in late April, and leaves in late August.

Robin
Closely mirrors the Wren in breeding distribution, but differs from that species in being abundant as a winter visitor in coastal regions, as in most habitats everywhere.

Nightingale
A familiar breeding bird throughout the region, usually arriving in late March, and common passage migrant along the coast.

Bluethroat
Common winter visitor to reedbeds at many sites, often in quite high densities. The overwhelming majority are of the white-throated subspecies *cyanecula*, but birds showing characters of the blue throated, eastern *magna* form have been recorded on rare occasions.

Red-flanked Bluetail
An adult female was trapped at the Llobregat Delta in November 1998.

Black Redstart
Locally common breeding species, normally in rocky, mountainous areas, and abundant winter visitor to all parts.

Redstart
Very sparsely distributed breeding species of high valleys in Cataluña and the Sistema Ibérico. Regular passage migrant along the coast, sometimes occuring as early as February, and returning in October. Winter records exist.

Whinchat
A few pairs may still breed in the higher valleys of Cataluña – otherwise a common spring and autumn passage bird.

Stonechat
Common and apparently fairly sedentary in suitable habitat everywhere. A bird showing the characters of one of the eastern races was seen in the Ebro Delta in March 1997.

Northern Wheatear
The common breeding wheatear of the higher plateaux, such as in Teruel, and abundant passage migrant through the region.

Black-eared Wheatear
Common summer visitor, often occupying warmer slopes than the previous species, though their relative biologies are not fully clear, and both species may well be found in close proximity.

Black Wheatear
Common and sedentary resident of rocky ravines and cliffs, both on the coast and inland. Tends to drop down to coastal areas in winter, in colder parts of its range.

Rock Thrush
A bird of the higher mountains, so far as breeding is concerned, (usually, if not always, above 1,000 metres) and an occasional, solitary migrant at coastal locations.

Blue Rock Thrush
Common breeding resident of coastal and inland cliffs, castles, ruins, dams and the like. (Recently a pair has bred in an apartment-block in Benidorm!)

Ring Ouzel
Autumn and winter visitor in small numbers, occuring erratically, usually in hill areas.

Blackbird
Common resident of wooded and cultivated areas throughout. Also common passage migrant and winter visitor.

Fieldfare
Scarce and irregular winter visitor, normally to the north.

Song Thrush
Common breeding resident of Catalán woodlands – elsewhere a passage migrant and local wintering species, sometimes in large numbers.

Redwing
Regular migrant, especially in October/November, and local winter visitor to upland woods and olive groves.

Mistle Thrush
Locally common breeding species of many kinds of habitat, both montane and lowland. Also appears in areas where it does not breed, often in March and April.

Cetti's Warbler
As a breeding species, tends to be more common at sea-level in the northern half of the region, retiring to the higher streams in summer further south. Common in winter in all reedbeds.

Fan-tailed Warbler
Common resident of reedy waters, ditches and damper fields throughout. Some are sedentary, but numbers appear to be reduced outside the breeding season, and some certainly emigrate to Africa.

Grasshopper Warbler
Rare but annual migrant, which has bred sporadically at Aiguamolls and the Ebro Delta.

Savi's Warbler
Very sparsely distributed breeding visitor, often arriving early in March, and breeding principally at the Albufera, Marjal del Moro and the Ebro Delta.

Moustached Warbler
This sedentary warbler breeds at practically all wetlands covered in this guide. Often most easily located in winter, when the similar song of the commoner Reed Warbler is absent.

Aquatic Warbler
Rare but probably annual passage migrant, usually in April or September, along the coast, most often discovered by ringers!

Sedge Warbler
Rather more frequent than the last species, but also most likely to turn up in mist-nets.

Marsh Warbler
This species completes the trio (with the previous two) of irregular migrants, and may well be the scarcest of them, as records are confused by the difficulty of separating this species from the next.

Reed Warbler
Abundant summer visitor and passage migrant to all suitable wetlands. A worrying hybrid Reed x Great Reed Warbler was trapped in the Ebro Delta in 1996.

Great Reed Warbler
Common summer visitor and passage migrant, often preferring high stands of reeds.

Paddyfield Warbler
One was trapped at El Hondo in March 1998.

Olivaceous Warbler
A very local breeding species, whose strongest concentration is in the valleys in the hinterland of Valencia and southern Castellón. Also seen on passage at coastal sites, usually in May and September.

Icterine Warbler
A 'ringers' bird', more-or-less annual, usually on the Columbretes, in May.

Melodious Warbler
A numerous breeding visitor to streamside thickets throughout. Also a common migrant, normally in May and September.

Sardinian Warbler

Marmora's Warbler
If all records of this surprisingly difficult bird had been accepted, it would appear to be fairly frequent. However, all but a May 1997 singing male from Barcelona have been rejected, even including some of birds examined in the hand. You have been warned! Recent separation of this super-species into Marmora's Warbler and Balearic Warbler does little to help, and it is clear from many of the photographs which accompany the relevant article in British Birds (ackn.) that the separation of these and the next species can scarcely be achieved with reliability in the field.

Dartford Warbler
Common breeding resident of matorral scrub, descending in numbers to occupy coastal sites in winter. Many birds also pass along the coast in spring and autumn.

Spectacled Warbler
Like the last species, a partial migrant, but with a generally more southerly distribution, and a liking for low, saline vegetation on salt-flats and the like. Breeds, although locally, at most suitable sites.

Subalpine Warbler
A summer visitor and passage migrant, often first appearing early in March. Normally breeds up to quite high altitudes, and in pines and higher scrub.

Sardinian Warbler
Abundant resident, becoming even more numerous in winter, when it is a familiar garden bird throughout.

Orphean Warbler
A scarce and local breeding visitor to open oak, and sometimes conifer, woods. Passes through on the northward journey in May.

Lesser Whitethroat
A very rare passage migrant, which really needs to be verified in the hand unless studied closely.

Whitethroat
A breeding visitor and passage migrant, nesting being restricted mainly to higher hills in the south, but more widespread in Cataluña.

Garden Warbler
Breeds mainly in Barcelona, Girona and the upper river valleys of Teruel. Otherwise a regular passage migrant.

Blackcap
An abundant winter visitor, also breeding commonly on higher ground in Castellón, and throughout Cataluña.

Yellow-browed Warbler
Just a few October and November records exist, of this long-distance traveller, most referring to birds trapped at coastal locations.

Bonelli's Warbler
A breeding visitor to open montane woodlands throughout, nesting at lower altitudes in the northern areas. Arrives in late March and leaves in August, sometimes singing on passage.

Wood Warbler
A scarce migrant, typically found in April or May along the coast.

Chiffchaff
An abundant winter visitor to almost all habitats, particularly fond of reedbeds and gardens. Also a passage migrant.

Willow Warbler
Common passage migrant, just possibly breeding in the extreme northeast of our region.
Goldcrest
Breeds at the extreme northern limit of the region, in Pyrenean foothills. Otherwise a scarce winter visitor to northern parts, and exceptional further south, for example: one bird was seen at Santa Pola in early December 1998.

Firecrest
Breeding resident, mainly at higher altitudes in the south, dispersing in winter, when can be met with almost anywhere.

Spotted Flycatcher
A common breeding visitor of woodland, from mid-April to September.

Red-breasted Flycatcher
A rare autumn vagrant. This apart, two recent winters have seen the species overwintering, one frequenting a garden near Calpe, Alicante, during both winters, whilst another was trapped on El Hondo in October 1997, whilst yet another was seen the following September, at nearby El Pinet.

Collared Flycatcher
A female was trapped and ringed at Aiguamolls in May 1997. The only previous record was an autumn bird, trapped in the Ebro Delta in 1994.

Pied Flycatcher
A scarce and local breeding species in the upland valleys of the Sistema Ibérico. Otherwise a common passage migrant along our coast.

Bearded Tit
A very sparsely distributed breeding bird, limited to the larger coastal wetlands. Appears to be largely sedentary.

Long-tailed Tit
Common and well distributed in woodland and garden habitats throughout, dispersive outside the breeding season.

Marsh Tit
Just creeps into our area as a breeding species in the far northeast of Cataluña, where it is found in the Pyrenean foothills.

Crested Tit
Common and sedentary in pinewoods, but scarce at low altitudes in the south.

Coal Tit
A common resident of pines practically everywhere though much scarcer at sea-level in the south.

Blue Tit
Abundant in northern parts of the region, occupying many habitats. Much less common in the south, and virtually absent from the Province of Alicante.

Great Tit
An abundant resident throughout.

Golden Oriole

Nuthatch
Resident in the wooded hillsides and valleys of the Sistema Ibérico and the Pyrenean foothills.

Wallcreeper
A scarce and irregular winter wanderer to rocky canyons and cliff-faces virtually anywhere, being recorded regularly in the Maestrazgo, for example. More likely to be found the higher you advance towards the Pyrenees.

Treecreeper
This northern species, occuring in the higher Pyrenean valleys, is represented by a small isolated population in oakwoods in Barcelona Province.

Short-toed Treecreeper
Widely and commonly distributed in woodland of many types, though typical of mature pinewoods.

Penduline Tit
Very common (though discreet) as a breeding species in the Ebro valley, and at wetlands in Cataluña. Elsewhere scarce, though much more easily found in winter, when it is a common visitor to coastal wetlands everywhere.

Golden Oriole
A common summer visitor to many types of woodland, though favouring riverine poplar stands and copses amidst cereal crops. Present from April to September.

Red-backed Shrike
A rare migrant for most of the region, most usually being found at coastal and island sites. A few breed, however, in Girona Province, in open woodland and thorn-scrub.

Lesser Grey Shrike
A speciality of Aiguamolls and its hinterland (some 6 pairs), breeding in few other places in Spain, apart from an isolated population on the borders of Lleida and Zaragoza Provinces. Attempted breeding has, however, been recorded in Cataluña and in Castellón Province. Elsewhere a very scarce migrant.

Great Grey Shrike
The Iberian subspecies *L.e.meridionalis*, considered by many to be a separate species, is common and well distributed everywhere. Numbers may well be augmented from the north in winter, when other forms may well be present, but further study is required.

Woodchat Shrike
A common though declining summer visitor, normally present in open woodland and plantations from April to September, though records outside these dates are not unknown.

Jay
Common in woodlands of Cataluña, becoming scarcer further south, where it is more likely to be found at high altitudes.

Azure-winged Magpie
This species has an overwhelmingly westerly distribution, largely confined to the drainage areas of the westerly-running rivers, but has occurred in Cataluña and Valencia, as well as Albacete. Winter flocks do wander, so it is not an impossible future colonist.

Magpie
Common resident of most of the region, unaccountably absent from the lowlands of Alicante.

Alpine Chough
Pyrenean birds may wander into the extreme north of our region, around the French border, where coastal observations have been made.

Chough

Chough
A numerous resident of rocky mountains almost anywhere, common in the Maestrazgo and the Sierras of Valencia and Alicante.

Jackdaw
Locally common throughout the region, inhabiting many types of natural and urban habitat.

Rook
In very occasional winters, groups – sometimes sizeable, *viz* 70 birds in Girona, in November 1996 – may wander this far from their normal haunts in France.

Carrion Crow
A common resident of northern areas, becoming much more scarce in the south, and absent from Alicante.

Raven
A common resident of hills and mountains everywhere, especially around cliffs and crags.

Starling
A breeding resident of Cataluña (mainly Girona and Barcelona Provinces, but with an outpost in the Delta of the Ebro), and abundant winter visitor, sometimes, as in Valencia city, forming flocks of several thousand birds.

Spotless Starling
Common breeding resident in all areas not occupied by the previous species. Less inclined to form large flocks outside the breeding season.

Rosy Starling
There have been to date less than ten records of this eastern vagrant, mostly in winter at coastal sites.

House Sparrow
Ubiquitous resident of virtually all areas.

Spanish Sparrow
Appears to have bred on the plains of Castellón until around 1970. The Atlas of the Breeding Birds of Spain shows records from Alicante and one or two other sites, but it seems likely that these sites are no longer occupied – if, indeed, they were then! An adult male was, however, seen near Tibi, Alicante, in March 2000. The identification of this species is not as straightforward as it may seem, and the possible complication of hybrids should not be ignored. May well, however, be on the increase, and is to be watched for.

Tree Sparrow
This local and declining species is most frequent on the coastal plains of Valencia and Castellón, but small flocks may be met with almost anywhere, with larger groups probable in winter.

Rock Sparrow
A well-distributed but local, and sometimes rather elusive species, perhaps easiest to locate on the uplands of Teruel.

Common Waxbill
This originally-introduced little finch breeds ferally in many parts of Iberia, and is to be sought around reedbeds, although it is erratic in occurrence, small flocks tending to breed for a few years and then move on.

Avadavat
Another species, like the last, originating from captive stock, and now appearing in wetland areas, though not so commonly as in western Iberia.

Red-eyed Vireo
1996 saw two widely-spaced records of this American vagrant, in Tarragona and in Elche, both at the end of October.

Chaffinch
Common breeding species, shunning the southern lowlands, but flocking everywhere in the winter months.

Brambling
A scarce winter visitor, often appearing in ones and twos in flocks of the previous species. Larger numbers occur further north, e.g. 48 at Aiguamolls in December 1996.

Serin
Abundant breeding resident of orchards, pinewoods and citrus plantations, at almost any altitude.

May arguably be the most numerous bird in the region, although reported to be in decline in Barcelona parks.

Citril Finch
In our region, the sole breeding outpost is a small one, in the upper parts of the Sistema Ibérico.

In winter, birds occasionally wander to lower levels.

Greenfinch
A very common resident throughout. Like other seemingly sedentary species, its occasional appearance on the Columbretes suggests some migrational movement.

Goldfinch
Very common resident of the entire region.

Siskin
As a breeding bird, restricted to high pinewoods in the Sistema Ibérico. Winters widely throughout the region.

Linnet
Common resident in almost the whole region, only absent from some coastal lowlands, at least during the nesting season.

Crossbill
Resident and irruptive wanderer throughout, breeding being dependent for its timing and locality upon the emergence and abundance of its favourite pine-seeds.

Trumpeter Finch
This relatively recent addition to the Spanish avifauna breeds somewhat to the south of our area, in the dry barrancos of Almería. Wanderers, however, tend to show up just about annually, usually in Alicante Province where two small breeding populations became established by 2000, in arid barrancos near the capital.

Common Rosefinch
A fairly regular vagrant, most often encountered during trapping on the Columbretes, both in spring and autumn.

Bullfinch
Breeds in the woodland of Girona Province. A very rare winter vagrant elsewhere.

Hawfinch
A very scarce and erratic breeding species. More likely to be found as a winter or early spring wanderer, occasionally in groups.

Lapland Bunting
Extremely scarce autumn vagrant, so far only noted from the Columbretes.

Snow Bunting
A rare winter visitor, most often found along the coast.

Yellowhammer
Breeds at the extreme northern limit of our area, and occasionally wanders south in winter, when it has been met with as far south as northern Alicante.

Cirl Bunting
Common breeding resident of sunny, wooded, hillsides throughout.

Rock Bunting
Probably more widespread than the last species, breeding at a variety of altitudes, and utilising many habitats.

Ortolan Bunting
Largely restricted to the higher ground of the Sistema Ibérico as a breeding bird, preferring dry hillsides. A scarce migrant elsewhere.

Little Bunting
The Columbretes, again, 'corners the market' for this autumn vagrant, with no more than two records at the time of writing, but 1996 saw an April record at Aiguamolls.

Reed Bunting
A very scarce breeding species, here at the southern extremity of its range, and only nesting regularly at wetlands from the Albufera de Valencia northwards. In winter, a common visitor to wetlands.

Pallas's Reed Bunting
A female was reported at Llobregat in April 1996, and will be Spain's first, if accepted.

Corn Bunting
An abundant resident of almost all open habitats, flocking and wandering outside the breeding season.

NOTE: Although the foregoing list includes several 'feral' species, a large number have been ignored, and it is now unusual to pass a week's birding, especially along the coast, without coming across at least one 'oddity' – ranging from a wide variety of parrots to mynahs, canaries and weavers, to a vast range of wildfowl and the odd Marabou Stork! The foregoing list is by no means 'official' – but rather reflects the authors' views as to the provenance, or at least probability, of 'wildness.'

Checklist

					English name	Scientific name
					Red-throated Diver	*Gavia stellata*
					Black-throated Diver	*Gavia arctica*
					Great Northern Diver	*Gavia immer*
					Little Grebe	*Tachybaptus ruficollis*
					Great Crested Grebe	*Podiceps cristatus*
					Slavonian Grebe	*Podiceps auritus*
					Black-necked Grebe	*Podiceps nigricollis*
					Mediterranean Shearwater	*Puffinus mauretanicus*
					Yelkoiuan Shearwater	*Puffinus yelkouan*
					European Storm Petrel	*Hydrobates pelagicus*
					Swinhoe's Petrel	*Oceanodroma monorhis*
					Masked Booby	*Sula dactylatra*
					Northern Gannet	*Sula bassana*
					Cape Gannet	*Sula capensis*
					Great Cormorant	*Phalacrocorax carbo*
					European Shag	*Phalacrocorax aristotelis*
					Great Bittern	*Botaurus stellaris*
					Little Bittern	*Ixobrychus minutus*
					Black-crowned Night Heron	*Nycticorax nycticorax*
					Squacco Heron	*Ardeola ralloides*
					Cattle Egret	*Bubulcus ibis*
					Western Reef Egret	*Egretta gularis*
					Little Egret	*Egretta garzetta*
					Great White Egret	*Egretta alba*
					Grey Heron	*Ardea cinerea*
					Purple Heron	*Ardea purpurea*
					Black Stork	*Ciconia nigra*
					White Stork	*Ciconia ciconia*
					Glossy Ibis	*Plegadis falcinellus*
					Eurasian Spoonbill	*Platalea leucorodia*
					Greater Flamingo	*Phoenicopterus ruber*
					Lesser Flamingo	*Phoenicopterus minor*
					Mute Swan	*Cygnus olor*
					Bean Goose	*Anser fabalis*
					Greylag Goose	*Anser Anser*
					Egyptian Goose	*Alopochen aegyptiacus*
					Ruddy Shelduck	*Tadorna ferruginea*
					Common Shelduck	*Tadorna tadorna*
					American Wood Duck	*Aix sponsa*
					Mandarin Duck	*Aix galericulata*
					Eurasian Wigeon	*Anas penelope*
					Gadwall	*Anas strepera*
					Common Teal	*Anas crecca*
					Mallard	*Anas platyrhynchos*
					Northern Pintail	*Anas acuta*
					Garganey	*Anas querquedula*
					Blue-winged Teal	*Anas discors*
					Northern Shoveler	*Anas clypeata*
					Marbled Duck	*Marmaronetta angustirostris*
					Red-crested Pochard	*Netta rufina*
					Common Pochard	*Aythya ferina*

				English name	Scientific name
				Ring-necked Duck	*Aythya collaris*
				Ferruginous Duck	*Aythya nyroca*
				Tufted Duck	*Aythya fuligula*
				Greater Scaup	*Aythya marila*
				Common Eider	*Somateria mollissima*
				Long-tailed Duck	*Clangula hyemalis*
				Common Scoter	*Melanitta nigra*
				Velvet Scoter	*Melanitta fusca*
				Common Goldeneye	*Bucephala clangula*
				Smew	*Mergus albellus*
				Red-breasted Merganser	*Mergus serrator*
				Goosander	*Mergus merganser*
				Ruddy Duck	*Oxyura jamaicensis*
				White-headed Duck	*Oxyura leucocephala*
				European Honey Buzzard	*Pernis apivorus*
				Black-shouldered Kite	*Elanus caeruleus*
				Black Kite	*Milvus migrans*
				Red Kite	*Milvus milvus*
				Lammergeier	*Gypaetus barbatus*
				Egyptian Vulture	*Neophron percnopterus*
				Eurasian Griffon Vulture	*Gyps fulvus*
				Monk Vulture	*Aegypius monachus*
				Short-toed Eagle	*Circaetus gallicus*
				Western Marsh Harrier	*Circus aeruginosus*
				Hen Harrier	*Circus cyaneus*
				Pallid Harrier	*Circus macrourus*
				Montagu's Harrier	*Circus pygargus*
				Northern Goshawk	*Accipiter gentilis*
				Eurasian Sparrowhawk	*Accipiter nisus*
				Common Buzzard	*Buteo buteo*
				Long-legged Buzzard	*Buteo rufinus*
				Rough-legged Buzzard	*Buteo lagopus*
				Lesser Spotted Eagle	*Aquila pomarina*
				Spotted Eagle	*Aquila clanga*
				Tawny Eagle	*Aquila rapax*
				Spanish Imperial Eagle	*Aquila adalberti*
				Golden Eagle	*Aquila chrysaetos*
				Booted Eagle	*Hieraaetus pennatus*
				Bonelli's Eagle	*Hieraaetus fasciatus*
				Osprey	*Pandion haliaetus*
				Lesser Kestrel	*Falco naumanni*
				Common Kestrel	*Falco tinnunculus*
				Red-footed Kestrel	*Falco vespertinus*
				Merlin	*Falco columbarius*
				Eurasian Hobby	*Falco subbuteo*
				Eleonora's Falcon	*Falco eleonorae*
				Peregrine Falcon	*Falco peregrinus*
				Rock Ptarmigan	*Lagopus mutus*
				Western Capercaillie	*Tetrao urogallus*
				Red-legged Partridge	*Alectoris rufa*
				Great Partridge	*Perdix perdix*

					English name	Scientific name
					Common Quail	*Coturnix coturnix*
					Common Pheasant	*Phasianus colchicus*
					Water Rail	*Rallus aquaticus*
					Spotted Crake	*Porzana porzana*
					Little Crake	*Porzana parva*
					Baillon's Crake	*Porzana pusilla*
					Corn Crake	*Crex crex*
					Common Moorhen	*Gallinula chloropus*
					Purple Swamp-hen	*Porphyrio porphyrio*
					Common Coot	*Fulica atra*
					Red-knobbed Coot	*Fulica cristata*
					Common Crane	*Grus grus*
					Demoiselle Crane	*Anthropoides virgo*
					Little Bustard	*Tetrax tetrax*
					Great Bustard	*Otis tarda*
					Eurasian Oystercatcher	*Haematopus ostralegus*
					Black-winged Stilt	*Himantopus himantopus*
					Pied Avocet	*Recurvirostra avosetta*
					Stone Curlew	*Burhinus oedicnemus*
					Collared Pratincole	*Glareola pratincola*
					Little Ringed Plover	*Charadrius dubius*
					Great Ringed Plover	*Charadrius hiaticula*
					Semipalmated Plover	*Charadrius semipalmatus*
					Kentish Plover	*Charadrius alexandrinus*
					Mountain Dotterel	*Charadrius morinellus*
					European Golden Plover	*Pluvialis apricaria*
					Grey Plover	*Pluvialis squatarola*
					Northern Lapwing	*Vanellus vanellus*
					Red Knot	*Calidris canutus*
					Sanderling	*Calidris alba*
					Little Stint	*Calidris minuta*
					Temminck's Stint	*Calidris temminckii*
					Pectoral Sandpiper	*Calidris melanotos*
					Curlew Sandpiper	*Calidris ferruginea*
					Purple Sandpiper	*Calidris maritima*
					Dunlin	*Calidris alpina*
					Broad-billed Sandpiper	*Limicola falcinellus*
					Ruff	*Philomachus pugnax*
					Jack Snipe	*Lymnocryptes minimus*
					Common Snipe	*Gallinago gallinago*
					Great Snipe	*Gallinago media*
					Long-billed Dowitcher	*Limnodromus scolopaceus*
					Eurasian Woodcock	*Scolopax rusticola*
					Black-tailed Godwit	*Limosa limosa*
					Bar-tailed Godwit	*Limosa lapponica*
					Whimbrel	*Numenius phaeopus*
					Eurasian Curlew	*Numenius arquata*
					Spotted Redshank	*Tringa erythropus*
					Common Redshank	*Tringa totanus*
					Marsh Sandpiper	*Tringa stagnatilis*
					Common Greenshank	*Tringa nebularia*

					English name	Scientific name
					Green Sandpiper	*Tringa ochropus*
					Wood Sandpiper	*Tringa glareola*
					Terek Sandpiper	*Xenus cinereus*
					Common Sandpiper	*Actitis hypoleucos*
					Spotted Sandpiper	*Actitis macularia*
					Ruddy Turnstone	*Arenaria interpres*
					Wilson's Phalarope	*Phalaropus tricolor*
					Red-necked Phalarope	*Phalaropus lobatus*
					Grey Phalarope	*Phalaropus fulicarius*
					Pomarine Skua	*Stercorarius pomarinus*
					Arctic Skua	*Stercorarius parasiticus*
					Long-tailed Skua	*Stercorarius longicaudus*
					Great Skua	*Stercorarius skua*
					Mediterranean Gull	*Larus melanocephalus*
					Laughing Gull	*Larus atricilla*
					Little Gull	*Larus minutus*
					Sabine Gull	*Larus sabini*
					Bonaparte's Gull	*Larus philadelphia*
					Black-headed Gull	*Larus ridibundus*
					Slender-billed Gull	*Larus genei*
					Audouin's Gull	*Larus audouinii*
					Ring-billed Gull	*Larus delawarensis*
					Common Gull	*Larus canus*
					Lesser Black-backed Gull	*Larus fuscus*
					Herring Gull	*Larus argentatus*
					Yellow-legged Gull	*Larus cachinnans*
					Iceland Gull	*Larus glaucoides*
					Glaucous Gull	*Larus hyperboreus*
					Great Black-backed Gull	*Larus marinus*
					Black-legged Kittiwake	*Rissa tridactyla*
					Gull-billed Tern	*Gelochelidon nilotica*
					Caspian Tern	*Sterna caspia*
					Royal Tern	*Sterna maxima*
					Lesser Crested Tern	*Sterna bengalensis*
					Sandwich Tern	*Sterna sandvicensis*
					Roseate Tern	*Sterna dougallii*
					Common Tern	*Sterna hirundo*
					Arctic Tern	*Sterna paradisaea*
					Little Tern	*Sterna albifrons*
					Whiskered Tern	*Chlidonias hybridus*
					Black Tern	*Chlidonias niger*
					White-winged Black Tern	*Chlidonias leucopterus*
					Common Guillemot	*Uria aalge*
					Razorbill	*Alca torda*
					Little Auk	*Alle alle*
					Atlantic Puffin	*Fratercula artica*
					Black-bellied Sandgrouse	*Pterocles orientalis*
					Pin-tailed Sandgrouse	*Pterocles alchata*
					Rock Dove	*Columba livia*
					Stock Dove	*Columba oenas*
					Common Wood Pigeon	*Columba palumbus*

					English name	Scientific name
					Collared Dove	*Streptopelia decaocto*
					Barbary Dove	*Streptopelia risoria*
					European Turtle Dove	*Streptopelia turtur*
					Monk Parakeet	*Myiopsitta monachus*
					Rose-ringed Parakeet	*Psittacula krameri*
					Great Spotted Cuckoo	*Clamator glandarius*
					Common Cuckoo	*Cuculus Canorus*
					Barn Owl	*Tyto alba*
					Eurasian Scops Owl	*Otus scops*
					Eagle Owl	*Bubo bubo*
					Little Owl	*Athene noctua*
					Tawny Owl	*Strix aluco*
					Long-eared Owl	*Asio otus*
					Short-eared Owl	*Asio flammeus*
					Tengmalm's Owl	*Aegolius funereus*
					European Nightjar	*Caprimulgus europaeus*
					Red-necked Nightjar	*Caprimulgus ruficollis*
					Common Swift	*Apus apus*
					Pallid Swift	*Apus pallidus*
					Alpine Swift	*Apus melba*
					Common Kingfisher	*Alcedo atthis*
					European Bee-eater	*Merops apiaster*
					European Roller	*Coracias garrulus*
					Hoopoe	*Upupa epops*
					Eurasian Wryneck	*Jynx torquilla*
					Green Woodpecker	*Picus viridis*
					Black Woodpecker	*Dryocopus martius*
					Great Spotted Woodpecker	*Dendrocopos major*
					Dupont's Lark	*Chersophilus duponti*
					Calandra Lark	*Melanocorypha calandra*
					Short-toed Lark	*Calandrella brachydactyla*
					Lesser Short-toed Lark	*Calandrella rufescens*
					Crested Lark	*Galerida cristata*
					Thekla Lark	*Galerida theklae*
					Wood Lark	*Lullula arborea*
					Sky Lark	*Alauda arvensis*
					Sand Martin	*Riparia riparia*
					Eurasian Crag Martin	*Ptyonoprogne rupestris*
					Barn Swallow	*Hirundo rustica*
					Red-rumped Swallow	*Hirundo daurica*
					House Martin	*Delichon urbica*
					Richard's Pipit	*Anthus novaeseelandiae*
					Tawny Pipit	*Anthus campestris*
					Tree Pipit	*Anthus trivialis*
					Meadow Pipit	*Anthus pratensis*
					Red-throated Pipit	*Anthus cervinus*
					Rock Pipit	*Anthus petrosus*
					Water Pipit	*Anthus spinoletta*
					Yellow Wagtail	*Motacilla flava*
					Grey Wagtail	*Motacilla cinerea*
					Pied Wagtail	*Motacilla alba*

English name	Scientific name
White-throated Dipper	*Cinclus cinclus*
Winter Wren	*Troglodytes troglodytes*
Hedge Accentor	*Prunella modularis*
Alpine Accentor	*Prunella collaris*
Rufous-tailed Scrub-robin	*Cercotrichas galactotes*
European Robin	*Erithacus rubecula*
Rufous Nightingale	*Luscinia megarhynchos*
Bluethroat	*Luscinia svecica*
Black Redstart	*Phoenicurus ochruros*
Common Redstart	*Phoenicurus phoenicurus*
Whinchat	*Saxicola rubetra*
Common Stonechat	*Saxicola torquata*
Northern Wheatear	*Oenanthe oenanthe*
Black-eared Wheatear	*Oenanthe hispanica*
Black Wheatear	*Oenanthe leucura*
Rufous-tailed Rock Thrush	*Monticola saxatilis*
Blue Rock Thrush	*Monticola solitarius*
Ring Ouzel	*Turdus torquatus*
Common Blackbird	*Turdus merula*
Fieldfare	*Turdus pilaris*
Song Thrush	*Turdus philomelos*
Redwing	*Turdus iliacus*
Mistle Thrush	*Turdus viscivorus*
Cetti's Warbler	*Cettia cetti*
Zitting Cisticola	*Cisticola juncidis*
Common Grasshopper Warbler	*Locustella naevia*
Savi's Warbler	*Locustella luscinioides*
Moustached Warbler	*Acrocephalus melannopogon*
Aquatic Warbler	*Acrocephalus paludicola*
Sedge Warbler	*Acrocephalus schoenobaenus*
Marsh Warbler	*Acrocephalus palustris*
Eurasian Reed Warbler	*Acrocephalus scirpaceus*
Great Reed Warbler	*Acrocephalus arundinaceus*
Paddyfield Warbler	*Acrocephalus agricola*
Olivaceous Warbler	*Hippolais pallida*
Melodious Warbler	*Hippolais polyglotta*
Marmora's Warbler	*Sylvia sarda*
Dartford Warbler	*Sylvia undata*
Spectacled Warbler	*Sylvia conspicillata*
Subalpine Warbler	*Sylvia cantillans*
Sardinian Warbler	*Sylvia melanocephala*
Orphean Warbler	*Sylvia hortensis*
Barred Warbler	*Sylvia nisoria*
Lesser Whitethroat	*Sylvia curruca*
Common Whitethroat	*Sylvia communis*
Garden Warbler	*Sylvia borin*
Blackcap	*Sylvia atricapilla*
Bonelli's Warbler	*Phylloscopus bonelli*
Wood Warbler	*Phylloscopus sibilatrix*
Common Chiffchaff	*Phylloscopus collybita*
Willow Warbler	*Phylloscopus trochilus*

					English name	Scientific name
					Goldcrest	*Regulus regulus*
					Firecrest	*Regulus ignicapillus*
					Spotted Flycatcher	*Muscicapa striata*
					Red-breasted Flycatcher	*Ficedula parva*
					Collared Flycatcher	*Ficedula albicollis*
					Pied Flycatcher	*Ficedula hypoleuca*
					Bearded Tit	*Panurus biarmicus*
					Long-tailed Tit	*Aegithalos caudatus*
					Marsh Tit	*Parus palustris*
					Crested Tit	*Parus cristatus*
					Coal Tit	*Parus ater*
					Blue Tit	*Parus caeruleus*
					Great Tit	*Parus major*
					Wood Nuthatch	*Sitta europaea*
					Wallcreeper	*Tichodroma muraria*
					Eurasian Treecreeper	*Certhia familiaris*
					Short-toed Treecreeper	*Certhia brachydactyla*
					Eurasian Penduline Tit	*Remiz pendulinus*
					Eurasian Golden Oriole	*Oriolus oriolus*
					Red-backed Shrike	*Lanius collurio*
					Lesser Grey Shrike	*Lanius minor*
					Great Grey Shrike	*Lanius excubitor*
					Woodchat Shrike	*Lanius senator*
					Eurasian Jay	*Garrulus glandarius*
					Azure-winged Magpie	*Cyanopica cyana*
					Black-billed Magpie	*Pica pica*
					Spotted Nutcracker	*Nucifraga caryocatactes*
					Yellow-billed Chough	*Pyrrhocorax graculus*
					Red-billed Chough	*Pyrrhocorax pyrrhocorax*
					Eurasian Jackdaw	*Corvus monedula*
					Rook	*Corvus frugilegus*
					Carrion Crow	*Corvus corone*
					Common Raven	*Corvus corax*
					Common Starling	*Sturnus vulgaris*
					Spotless Staring	*Sturnus unicolor*
					Rosy Starling	*Sturnus roseus*
					House Sparrow	*Passer domesticus*
					Spanish Sparrow	*Passer hispaniolensis*
					Eurasian Tree Sparrow	*Passer montanus*
					Rock Sparrow	*Petronia petronia*
					White-winged Snowfinch	*Montifringilla nivalis*
					Common Waxbill	*Estrilda astrild*
					Red Avadavat	*Amandava amandava*
					Copmmon Chaffinch	*Fringilla coelebs*
					Brambling	*Fringilla montifringilla*
					Citril Finch	*Serinus citrinella*
					European Greenfinch	*Carduelis chloris*
					European Goldfinch	*Carduelis carduelis*
					European Siskin	*Carduelis spinus*
					Common Linnet	*Carduelis cannabina*
					Common Crossbill	*Loxia curvirostra*

					English name	Scientific name
					Trumpeter Finch	*Bucanetes githagineus*
					Common Rosefinch	*Carpodacus erythrinus*
					Common Bullfinch	*Pyrrhula pyrrhula*
					Hawfinch	*Coccothraustes coccothraustes*
					Lapland Longspur	*Calcarius lapponicus*
					Snow Bunting	*Plectrophenax nivalis*
					Yellowhammer	*Emberiza citrinella*
					Cirl Bunting	*Emberiza cirlus*
					Rock Bunting	*Emberiza cia*
					Ortolan Bunting	*Emberiza hortulana*
					Reed Bunting	*Emberiza schoeniclus*
					Black-headed Bunting	*Emberiza melanocephala*
					Corn Bunting	*Miliaria calandra*

NOTES

NOTES

NOTES

NOTES